T0093123

Cyber Security and Operations Management for Industry 4.0

This book seamlessly connects the topics of Industry 4.0 and cyber security. It discusses the risks and solutions of using cyber security techniques for Industry 4.0.

Cyber Security and Operations Management for Industry 4.0 covers the cyber security risks involved in the integration of Industry 4.0 into businesses and highlights the issues and solutions. The book offers the latest theoretical and practical research in the management of cyber security issues common in Industry 4.0 and also discusses the ethical and legal perspectives of incorporating cyber security techniques and applications into the day-to-day functions of an organization. Industrial management topics related to smart factories, operations research, and value chains are also discussed.

This book is ideal for industry professionals, researchers, and those in academia who are interested in learning more about how cyber security and Industry 4.0 are related and can work together.

Cyber Security and Operations Management for Industry 4.0

Edited by
Ahmed A. Elngar
N. Thillaiarasu
Mohamed Elhoseny
K. Martin Sagayam

CRC Press
Taylor & Francis Group
Boca Raton London New York

CRC Press is an imprint of the
Taylor & Francis Group, an **informa** business

First edition published 2023
by CRC Press
6000 Broken Sound Parkway NW, Suite 300, Boca Raton, FL 33487-2742

and by CRC Press
2 Park Square, Milton Park, Abingdon, Oxon, OX14 4RN

Library of Congress Cataloging-in-Publication Data
Names: Elngar, Ahmed A., editor. | Thillaiarasu, N., editor. | Elhoseny, Mohamed, editor. |
Sagayam, K. Martin, 1987– editor.
Title: Cyber security and operations management for Industry 4.0 /
edited by Ahmed A. Elngar, N. Thillaiarasu, Mohamed Elhoseny, K. Martin Sagayam.
Description: Boca Raton : CRC Press, 2023 | Includes bibliographical references and index.
Identifiers: LCCN 2022030026 (print) | LCCN 2022030027 (ebook) |
ISBN 9781032079486 (paperback) | ISBN 9781032079479 (hardback) |
ISBN 9781003212201 (ebook)
Subjects: LCSH: Computer security–Management. | Industry 4.0
Classification: LCC QA76.9.A25 C918122 2023 (print) |
LCC QA76.9.A25 (ebook) | DDC 658.4/78–dc23/eng/20221006
LC record available at https://lccn.loc.gov/2022030026
LC ebook record available at https://lccn.loc.gov/2022030027

ISBN: 978-1-032-07947-9 (hbk)
ISBN: 978-1-032-07948-6 (pbk)
ISBN: 978-1-003-21220-1 (ebk)

DOI: 10.1201/9781003212201

Typeset in Times
by Newgen Publishing UK

Contents

PART 1   Cyber Security

PART 2   Industry 4.0

Preface

This book, entitled *Cyber Security and Operations Management for Industry 4.0*, consists of seven chapters. The book, which focuses on cyber security for modern engineering operations management toward intelligent industry, discusses cyber security risks and operations research, systems engineering, project management, and industry as they continue to evolve, in both quantity in the same domains as well as new types and ways of breaking into computing systems, software applications, websites, databases, programmable networks, and so on.

The aim of this book is to provide a forum for scientists, researchers, students, and practitioners to present their latest research results, ideas, developments, and applications in the areas of cybersecurity techniques, security challenges, and opportunities for emerging technologies such as cloud computing, Internet of Things (IoT), edge computing, big data, blockchain, artificial intelligence, machine learning (ML), 5G, mechanical systems engineering, electrical application, micro-machining, renewable energy, industrial and production engineering, additive manufacturing, and many others.

The book is organized into seven chapters and these are divided into two sections, which include the explanation of topics with discussion of relevant algorithms.

PART 1: CYBER SECURITY

Chapter 1 explains efficient deep learning techniques for security and privacy in industry.

Chapter 2 discusses crypto-based secure outbound supply chain authentication for Industry 4.0 in this chapter.

Chapter 3 contains the concept of a machine learning-based approach for fruit grading and classification.

PART 2: INDUSTRY 4.0

Chapter 4 discusses the fundamentals of artificial intelligence, which is used find the impact on pattern classification in association with IoT for advanced applications.

Chapter 5 focuses on a modified clonal selection algorithm based on a positive selection method in an accounting information system (AIS) to solve job shop scheduling problems.

Chapter 6 discusses IoT health-care devices for patient monitoring. It explains efficient deep learning techniques for security and privacy in industry.

Chapter 7 briefs readers about deep learning techniques used for detection of disease in tomato plants.

The book covers fundamental algorithms in security design, application security attacks and defenses, introduction to cryptography, cryptography in the field, foundations in the practice of symmetric encryption, public-key cryptography, advance primitives, internet protocols, network security, defenses and tools, denial of service attacks, injection and cross-domain attacks, web security, dealing with data breach attacks and defenses, cloud security, and privacy concerns.

MATLAB® is a registered trademark of The Math Works, Inc. For product information, please contact:

The Math Works, Inc.
3 Apple Hill Drive
Natick, MA 01760-2098
Tel: 508-647-7000
Fax: 508-647-7001
E-mail: info@mathworks.com
Web: http://www.mathworks.com

Editors

Ahmed A. Elngar is the founder and head of the Scientific Innovation Research Group (SIRG) and assistant professor of Computer Science in the Faculty of Computers and Information at Beni-Suef University. He is also the director of the Technological and Informatics Studies Center (TISC), Faculty of Computers and Information at Beni-Suef University. He is also the managing editor of *Journal of Cybersecurity and Information Management* (JCIM). Dr. Elngar has published more than 25 scientific research papers in prestigious international journals and over five books covering such diverse topics as data mining, intelligent systems, social networks, smart environment, and research works and publications. He is a collaborative researcher. He is a member of the Egyptian Mathematical Society (EMS) and the International Rough Set Society (IRSS). His other research areas include Internet of Things (IoT), network security, intrusion detection, machine learning, data mining, artificial intelligence, big data, authentication, cryptology, health-care systems, and automation systems. He has served as an editor and reviewer for many international journals around the world. Dr. Elngar has won several awards, including "Young Researcher in Computer Science Engineering," from Global Outreach Education Summit and Awards 2019, on January 31, 2019 (Thursday) in Delhi, India. Also, he received the "Best Young Researcher Award (Male) (Below 40 years)," Global Education and Corporate Leadership Awards (GECL-2018), Plot No-8, Shivaji Park, Alwar, Rajasthan-301001, India. In addition, he has an intellectual property right called "El Dahshan Authentication Protocol," Information Technology Industry Development Agency (ITIDA), Technical Report, 2016. Dr. Elngar is involved in many activities in the community and in environmental service, including organizing 12 workshops hosted by a large number of universities in almost all governorates of Egypt.

N. Thillaiarasu is currently an associate professor in the School of Computing and Information Technology at REVA University, Bangalore. He has also served as assistant professor at Galgotias University, Greater Noida, from July 2019 to December 2020. He held the position of assistant professor for seven years in the Department of Computer Science and Engineering at SNS College of Engineering, Coimbatore. Dr. Thillaiarasu earned his bachelor of engineering in Computer Science and Engineering from Selvam College of Technology in 2010 and received his master of engineering in Software Engineering from Anna University Regional Center, Coimbatore, in 2012. He received his PhD from Anna University, Chennai, in 2019, His areas of interest include cloud computing, security, IoT, and machine learning.

 **Mohamed Elhoseny** is currently an assistant professor in the Faculty of Computers and Information at Mansoura University. He was appointed as an ACM Distinguished Speaker from 2019 to 2022. Collectively, Dr. Elhoseny has authored/co-authored over 85 ISI-indexed journal articles in high-ranked and prestigious journals such as *IEEE Transactions on Industrial Informatics* (IEEE), *IEEE Transactions on Reliability* (IEEE), *Future Generation Computer Systems* (Elsevier), and *Neural Computing and Applications* (Springer). Additionally, he has authored/ edited 11 international books (nine published by Springer, one published by Taylor & Francis Group, and one published by Elsevier). His research interests include smart cities, network security, artificial intelligence, IoT, and intelligent systems. Dr. Elhoseny serves as editor-in-chief of *International Journal of Smart Sensor Technologies and Applications* (IGI Global). As well, he is associate editor of many journals such as *IEEE Journal of Biomedical and Health Informatics* (IEEE), *Access* (IEEE), *Scientific Reports* (Nature), *IEEE Future Directions* (IEEE), *Remote Sensing* (MDPI), *International Journal of E-services and Mobile Applications* (IGI Global), and *Applied Intelligence* (Springer). Dr. Elhoseny also served as the co-chair, the publication chair, the program chair, and a track chair for the proceedings of several international conferences published by IEEE and Springer. He is editor-in-Chief of the Studies in Distributed Intelligence Springer book series, Editor-in-chief of the Sensors Communication for Urban Intelligence CRC Press–Taylor & Francis Group book series, and editor-in-chief of the Distributed Sensing and Intelligent Systems CRC Press–Taylor & Francis Group book series. Dr. Elhoseny has been granted several awards by diverse funding bodies such as the Young Researcher Award in Artificial Intelligence from the Federation of Arab Scientific Research Councils in 2019, the Obada International Prize for Young Distinguished Scientists 2020, the Egypt National Prize for Young Researchers in 2018, the best PhD thesis at Mansoura University in 2015, the SRGE Best Young Researcher Award in 2017, and membership in the Egyptian Young Academy of Science (EYAS) in 2019. Moreover, he has been a TPC member or reviewer at over 50 international conferences and workshops. Furthermore, Dr. Elhoseny has reviewed papers for more than 80 international journals, including *IEEE Communications Magazine*, *IEEE Transactions on Intelligent Transportation Systems*, *IEEE Sensors Letters*, *IEEE Communication Letters*, *Elsevier Computer Communications*, *Computer Networks*, *Sustainable Cities and Society*, *Wireless Personal Communications*, and *Expert Systems with Applications*. He has been an invited guest on many media programs to comment on technologies and related issues.

K. Martin Sagayam received his PhD in Electronics and Communication Engineering (ECE) ("Signal Image Processing Using Machine Learning Algorithms") from Karunya University. He received a master of engineering in Communication Systems from Anna University, Chennai, and earned a bachelor of engineering in Electronics and Communication Engineering from Anna University. Currently, Dr. Sagayam is an assistant professor in the Department of ECE, Karunya Institute Technology and Sciences, Coimbatore, India. He has authored/co-authored many articles in refereed international journals. Dr. Sagayam has also presented more than 20 papers at reputed international and national conferences. He has authored two edited collections and ten book chapters with reputed international publishers like Elsevier, Springer, IGI Global, and CRC Press. Dr. Sagayam is a member of the editorial board for reputed books and book series with respected international publishers like IGI Global and CRC Press. He has reviewed research articles for the journals *Signal, Image and Video Processing*, *Intelligent Decision Technologies*, *International Journal of Engineering Research & Technology*, *Pattern Analysis and Its Applications*, and the Informing Science Institute. Dr. Sagayam is an active member of professional bodies such as Engineering and Scientific Research Groups, International Society of Promising Computer Engineers, Copernicus, Scientific Engineering Research Corporation, International Association of Computer Science and Information Technology, International Association of Engineers, Indian Society of Electronics and Communication Engineering, and ORCID. His areas of interest include communication systems, signal and image processing, machine learning and virtual reality.

Contributors

A. Diana Andrusia
Karunya Institute of Technology and
  Sciences
Coimbatore, India

Hien Dang
Thuy Loi University
Hanoi, Vietnam

A. Devi
REVA University
Bengaluru, India

T. Priya Radhika Devi
Mailam Engineering College
Mailam, India

R. Indumathi
Manakula Vinayagar Institute of
  Technology
Puducherry, India

K. Madhan
Mailam Engineering College
Mailam, India

Manjula Sanjay Koti
Dayananda Sagar Academy of
  Technology & Management
Bengaluru, India

M. Rajesh Kumar
Mailam Engineering College
Mailam, India

S. Satheesh Kumar
REVA University
Bengaluru, India

V. Vinoth Kumar
JAIN University
Bengaluru, India

I. Thusnavis Bella Mary
Karunya Institute of Technology and
  Sciences
Coimbatore, India

G. Manikandan
Kongu Engineering College
Perundurai, India

R. Murugesan
REVA University
Bengaluru, India

V. Muthukumaran
REVA University
Bengaluru, India

M. Narayanan
St. Martin's Engineering College
Secunderabad, India

T. Mary Neebha
Karunya Institute of Technology and
  Sciences
Coimbatore, India

N. Palanivel
Manakula Vinayagar Institute of
  Technology
Puducherry, India

A. Trephena Patricia
Panimalar Engineering College
Chennai, India

T. Poongothai
St. Martin's Engineering College
Secunderabad, India

S. Prasanna
Mailam Engineering College
Mailam, India

C.V. Rahav
Kongu Engineering College
Perundurai, India

V. Rajalakshmi
REVA University
Bangaluru, India

Gopal Rathinam
University of Buraimi
Al Buraimi, Oman

E.B. Priyanka S.
Kongu Engineering College
Perundurai, India

V. Selvi
Manakula Vinayagar Institute of
    Technology
Puducherry, India

B. Saravanan
Mailam Engineering College
Mailam, India

P. Sathiyanarayanan
Manakula Vinayagar Institute of
    Technology
Puducherry, India

S. Thangavel
Kongu Engineering College
Perundurai, India

M. Vijayaragavan
Mailam Engineering College
Mailam, India

Part 1

Cyber Security

1 Efficient Deep Learning Techniques for Security and Privacy in Industry

¹Manjula Sanjay Koti, ²V. Muthukumaran,
³A. Devi, ⁴V. Rajalakshmi, ⁵S. Satheesh Kumar,
and ⁶V. Vinoth Kumar
¹Dayananda Sagar Academy of Technology & Management,
Bengaluru, India
²Department of Mathematics, School of Applied Sciences,
REVA University, Bengaluru, India
³School of Computer Science and Applications,
REVA University, Bengaluru, India
⁴School of Commerce, REVA University, Bangalore, India
⁵Department of Computer Science, School of Applied
Sciences, REVA University, Bengaluru, India
⁶Department of Computer Science and Engineering,
JAIN University, Bengaluru, India

CONTENTS

1.1 Introduction 4
1.2 Deep Learning 5
    1.2.1 Deep Learning Techniques 6
    1.2.2 Supervised Learning..7
    1.2.3 Unsupervised Learning...7
        1.2.3.1 Clustering..7
        1.2.3.2 Association...8
        1.2.3.3 Dimensionality Reduction 8
    1.2.4 Semi-supervised Learning...8
    1.2.5 Reinforcement Learning..9
1.3 Deep Learning in Security and Privacy 9
1.4 Common Cyber Attack Terminology 11
    1.4.1 Spam Detection 11
    1.4.2 Intrusion Detection 12
    1.4.3 Malware Detection 12
1.5 Deep Learning Security and Privacy Challenges 13
    1.5.1 Model Extraction Attack 15
    1.5.2 Model Inversion Attack 15

DOI: 10.1201/9781003212201-2

1.1   INTRODUCTION

Using Internet services for both personnel and industry needs is unavoidable in the modern era as these services have transformed the world into a "global village." To offer and ensure security while availing these services has become a very tedious and most challenging task for academicians, researchers, and industrial experts. Over a decade, the size and scale of cyber attacks have seen exponential growth due to a number of factors including the growing trend of adopting digital infrastructure in industries and challenges in employing an adequate cyber security workforce [1, 2]. In the twenty-first century, cyber security faces serious economic and national security challenges in protecting critical infrastructures of government and industry, and the public from being attacked and from unauthorized access. Cyber attacks can possibly be seen as a modern digital war where physical weapons are not required, yet it is most dangerous as it exposes the information of individuals, business organizations, and a nation to disrupt their critical operations and functionalities in their domain. In the recent past, artificial intelligence (AI) has been growing by "leaps and bounds" across nine business functions in numerous industries, and this growth can potentially generate an annual value of between \$3.5T and \$5.8T in the coming years [3].

Considering this reality, many have wondered how cyber security professionals are going to address and tackle these issues to protect and defend their information from all forms of attack. Yes, there have been numerous methods and techniques adapted to protect this sensitive information from attackers; still, they were able to invade and modify or steal such information. Many experts have suggested considering machine learning (ML) approaches to defend and protect digital infrastructures [4, 5]. AI, a monolith technology, is diversified and unique with its subtechniques such as machine learning, deep learning, and deep reinforcement learning that make AI a "cutting-edge technology." The following questions need to be considered:

1.   Could machine learning be effective in protecting against and detecting cyber attacks?
2.   Could machine learning achieve a higher rate of detecting and intercepting attacks than traditional and current methods?
3.   Could machine learning be successful in the automatic detection of attacks by agents or in engaging an adversary?

4. Should experts and researchers consider machine learning as a transformational force in cyber defense or as just a buildup?

This chapter of the book aims to examine the literature on deep learning to provide and achieve security and privacy in various industries over a time, and also analyzes its potential in outplaying other methods and approaches. The chapter consists of five sections: In the section that follows, we introduce the aim and scope of deep learning methods in offering security to various industries of the business market.

1.2 DEEP LEARNING

The term "deep learning" is not new to audiences as everyone is aware that it is a branch of machine learning and a subset of AI in which a neural network is used to mimic the "human brain" with a set of input and output values that are interconnected through hidden layer(s). Deep learning does not require any special programming to do everything in order to process a large data with much processing power. Deep learning can be defined as "a particular kind of machine learning that achieves great power and flexibility by learning to represent the world as a nested hierarchy of concepts, with each concept defined in relation to simpler concepts, and more abstract representations computed in terms of less abstract ones." Deep learning has been used in various industrial applications such as finance, banking, healthcare, agriculture, and so on [6, 7] (Figure 1.1).

Billions of neurons in the human brain are represented as an artificial neural network (ANN), where neurons are represented as either nodes or neurons. Deep learning is "self-taught and unsupervised feature learning consisting of multiple intermediate hidden layers that process information and from it like human brain

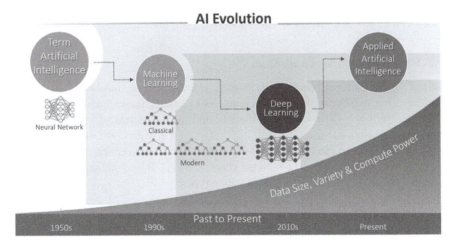

FIGURE 1.1 The evolution of artificial intelligence.

	Pre-1990s	1990s	2000s	2010s
SPAM DETECTION	1978: First spam email	Spam continues to worsen due to growth in email 1996: First spam blockers	2002: Machine learning methods first proposed for spam detection 2003: First attempts to regulate spam in the United States	Machine learning spam detection widely embedded in email services Emergence of deep learning-based classifiers
INTRUSION DETECTION	1980: First intrusion detection systems 1986: Anomaly detection systems combine expert rules and statistical analysis	Early 1990s: Neural networks for anomaly detection first proposed 1999: DARPA creates datasets to study intrusion detection systems	Machine learning further studied as a possible tool for misuse-based and anomaly-based intrusion detection	Late 2010s: Emergence of large-scale, cloud-based intrusion detection systems Deep learning studied for intrusion detection
MALWARE DETECTION	Early 1980s: First viruses found "in the wild" Late 1980s: First antivirus companies founded	Early 1990s: First polymorphic viruses 1996: IBM begins studying machine learning for malware detection	Early 2000s: First metamorphic viruses Wide number of traditional machine learning methods studied to detect malware	Rise of "next-gen" antivirus detection Emergence of ML-focused antivirus companies

FIGURE 1.2   The timeline of machine learning methods in security and privacy [4].

does," as described by Yoshua Bengio [9], and is mainly used to achieve the following with brain simulations:

- developing algorithms that are much effective and easier to use
- achieving revolutionary advances in AI and ML
- making use of a larger amount of data with the availability of fast enough computers
- achieving greater scalability by constructing larger neural networks and training them with more data to reach better performance by feeding more data
- performing automatic feature extraction through feature learning on raw data with more computation to train them [8, 9] (Figure 1.2).

1.2.1 DEEP LEARNING TECHNIQUES

Recent studies suggest that deep learning methods have outshined traditional methods such as Support Vector Machine (SVM), naive Bayes, random forests, k-means clustering, logistic regression models, and so on, in terms of findings and performance. "Traditional machine learning" refers to the wide range of old-fashioned methods that were an integral part of ML for decades until "deep learning" came into the picture for at least the past five to ten years [4, 9–11]. Based on functionality, deep learning algorithms are categorized into three types:

1. Supervised Learning
2. Unsupervised Learning
3. Semi-supervised Learning
4. Reinforcement Learning (Figure 1.3)

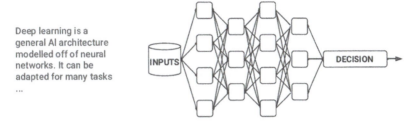

Deep learning is a general AI architecture modelled off of neural networks. It can be adapted for many tasks …

INPUTS DECISION

FIGURE 1.3 Deep learning examples architecture.

1.2.2 SUPERVISED LEARNING

In order to classify new inputs from the labeled data sets, a model is trained using these data sets to predict output with higher accuracy. A well-labeled data set on existing attacks would help in detecting future attacks just by matching the network traffic to the profile already known. Supervised learning can be widely used for *classification* and *regression* purposes while mining data. In *classification,* an algorithm is used to separate the data under specific categories based on its features. For example, a data set having the features of apples and oranges where it accurately predicts the output value, that is, either orange or apple, by processing input values. For an instance, Gmail is able to categorize whether the incoming message is valid or spam with the help of such algorithms. The most commonly used classification algorithms are support vector machine (SVM), random forest, decision trees, linear classifiers, and so on.

Regression uses an algorithm to identify and understand the "relationship between dependent and independent variables" based on different data points. These approaches are very useful in predicting numerical values with such data points, for example, predicting revenue projections of a given business. Linear regression, logistic regression, and polynomial regression are the most widely used regression techniques.

1.2.3 UNSUPERVISED LEARNING

Unsupervised learning helps in discovering hidden patterns from an unlabeled data set with an algorithm that analyzes and clusters the unlabeled data set with no form of human intervention. This approach is used to achieve the following tasks.

1.2.3.1 Clustering

Clustering is mainly used in market segmentation and image compression applications for grouping. Basically, it is a data mining approach to group unlabeled data either based on their similarities or differences. A k-means clustering algorithm is an example of this approach that forms groups with similar data points from the unlabeled data set, whereas a k-value algorithm helps in representing the size of those groups and its granularity.

1.2.3.2 Association

This method is mainly used in market basket analysis and recommendation engines to establish a relationship between the variables of an unlabeled data set using different sets of rules or association rules. For example, when purchasing a laptop online, the page will make recommendations to buy a laptop bag and other related accessories, or make suggestions with a message such as "Customers who bought this item also bought."

1.2.3.3 Dimensionality Reduction

This method is used when the features of a given unlabeled data set are very high, and it reduces those features into a manageable number without affecting the integrity of the original data. Preprocessing can be very effective with these methods in place, such as removing noise from an input image for better picture quality using auto-encoders.

1.2.4 SEMI-SUPERVISED LEARNING

Though data classification is a challenging task in supervised learning, the end results are trustworthy and accurate, whereas unsupervised learning lacks transparency in classifying and forming clusters from large volumes of unlabeled data and the results

TABLE 1.1

Difference Between Supervised and Unsupervised Learning [8, 10, 12]

Parameters	Supervised Learning	Unsupervised Learning
Goal	To predict outcomes for new data as the user knows the type of results to expect in up front	To get insights from a large unstructured volume of data by identifying dependent and independent features of it (hidden patterns)
Input Data	Algorithms are trained using well-structured data sets	Algorithms are used against an unstructured data set
Computational Complexity	Simple to implement and easy to use with programs like R or Python (Tensor Flow)	Complexity is high as it processes large sets of unclassified data
Time Complexity	Time-consuming and needs expertise in labeling input and output variables	Less time-consuming with inaccurate results and requires human intervention for validation of outcome
Accuracy	Delivers trustworthy and accurate results	Delivers moderate results with less accuracy
Applications	Spam detection, weather forecasting, sentiment analysis, etc.	Medical imaging, anomaly detection, recommendation engines etc.
Examples	Decision tree, linear regression, naive Bayes, support vector machine (SVM), etc.	Apriori algorithm, k-means clustering, k-nearest neighbor, etc.

might be inaccurate. To handle this problem, a semi-supervised learning approach uses both labeled and unlabeled data sets to extract the required features from them. This method yields better results in cases like a high volume of data that requires the intervention of both computers and humans. Medical image processing applications are a clean example of this method as it requires the help of both machines (CT scans) and radiologists for accurate predictions of a disease.

1.2.5 REINFORCEMENT LEARNING

Reinforcement learning is a machine learning model to make a sequence of decisions to maximize the rewards with machines and software in an environment that is potentially complex and uncertain. Unlike supervised learning, this approach has trained models with no answer key but the agent makes decisions to achieve the assigned task, that is, learn from mistakes, and a reinforcement technique learns from its experience when training a data set not available [13]. In simple terms, it works in sequential order where the input of the current stage is taken from the output of the previous input. That is, the decision is dependent. It is very effective in a game-like situation where the computer employs a trial-and-error technique using feedback from its own actions and experiences, and as a result either rewards or penalties are offered for the actions performed. Every action or event will result in either a *positive or a negative* effect on behavior. The main motive is to strengthen the behavior irrespective of a positive or a negative event. In addition, through the experience gathered by a reinforcement algorithm by thousands of trials, the machine's creativity can be improved. A chess game is a simple example of this technique. [14].

Figure 1.4 depicts the architecture of (a) reinforcement learning and (b) deep reinforcement learning. Preparing the simulation environment is one of the main difficulties in reinforcement learning such as being superhuman in chess, or driving an autonomous car becomes tricky in the real world. Another challenge is to communicate with the network since the system of rewards and penalties controls the agents of neural networks. Third, the agent performs its task as it is (in real time); thus, achieving local optimum in all situations and environments might be more challenging. Gaining rewards with no penalties has no meaning if the task is not completed [13, 15]. Q-learning and state-action-reward-state-action (SARSA) are the most commonly used algorithms with similar exploitation policies and different exploration strategies. To overcome the generality issue of these algorithms, deep q-networks (DQNs) and deep deterministic policy gradient (DDPG) were introduced. Reinforcement algorithms are widely used in applications like playing computer games and robotics and industrial automation [16].

1.3 DEEP LEARNING IN SECURITY AND PRIVACY

Over the last few decades, many deep learning algorithms have been majorly used in applications such as marketing, finance, sales, and so on. In early 2010, one could hardly come across a research study that targeted protecting products and businesses from malware and hacker attacks. However, some technology giants in business

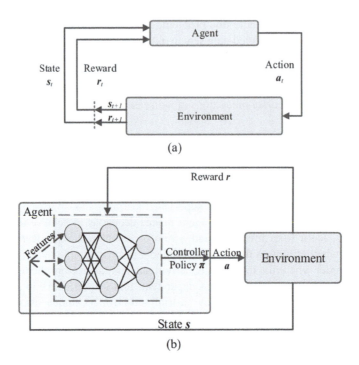

FIGURE 1.4 Reinforcement learning architecture.

such as Google, Microsoft, Salesforce, and Facebook have adapted deep learning based algorithms into their business products and services to ensure data security and privacy. Recently, Google infused such algorithms (TensorFlow, pytorch, keras) to catch "spam" emails missed by its Gmail filter. TensorFlow is used to detect typically difficult spam emails such as newly created domain messages, image-based emails, messages with hidden embedded content and so on [17, 18].

With ever emerging and increasing technological developments like data science and cloud computing, ensuring security and privacy of data over these platforms is a challenging task that requires the full attention of researchers and experts. The accuracy of deep learning algorithms mainly depends on the quality of labeled data sets that are not readily available in any platform.

Deep learning helps ensure security in the following ways:

1. Finding threats on a network with constant network traffic monitoring
2. Keeping people safe when browsing using "bad neighborhood" online
3. Providing end-point malware detection by matching the known malware behavior and attributes to detect unknown malware
4. Protecting data in the cloud by ensuring IP reputation analysis, location based analysis, and suspicious login activity
5. Detecting malware in encrypted traffic by pinpointing malicious patterns to find hidden threats in encryption [Cisco]

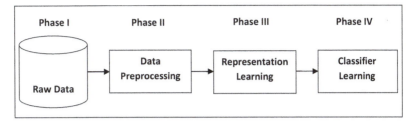

FIGURE 1.5   Deep learning: 4-phase workflow [26].

In the recent past, deep learning algorithms have shown significant improvements in the areas of malware detection and network intrusion detection over classic and rule-based machine learning algorithms [18].

In 1990–2010, many research investigations were carried out to ensure security over network data and information sharing using classic machine learning algorithms, but the results proved that such algorithms were not impactful in detecting security- and privacy-related attacks [19, 20]. Factually, the threats to both governmental and other business industries have seen exponential growth even in the presence of more capable technologies to detect them. Importantly, malicious attackers have capable resources and knowledge of advanced persistent threats, whereas cyber security professionals struggle to meet the ever-growing demand for expertise [21, 22]. Most businesses are not aware of the importance of keeping their IT infrastructure secure, particularly when stats signal that cyber attacks have grown from "several hundred to several million per day in some industries". Generally, an ML system generates alerts on suspicious behavior, automatically screens out potential attacks, and also detects anomalous activity [23, 24]. Yet, a few experts from the computer security community have made some remarks or challenges as follows:

1. The proposed system or algorithm must have a clear picture of what types of attack should be detected, through which a researcher can tailor such a system that is more specific, thus avoiding or reducing misclassifications in results.
2. The results might have serious flaws if one fails to establish strong relations between features and the attacks of interest when developing an algorithm or implanting a systematic approach [25] (Figure 1.5).

Deep learning can make these challenges much easier to overcome. Unlike traditional and classic machine learning algorithms, deep learning algorithms are less dependent on feature extraction and also result in higher accuracy with less domain knowledge [26].

1.4   COMMON CYBER ATTACK TERMINOLOGY

1.4.1   Spam Detection

In the early 2000s, spam was identified based on the IP address or keyword detection using probability association threshold value. When a risk reaches the preset threshold value, an email or message is identified as a spam and automatically blocked. The keywords could be words like "free" or "sex" or "lottery winner" and so on [27]. The core elements of spam detection remained the same over the years (treating all keywords as independent of one another) until better spam classifiers were introduced by researchers and experts to extract technical details from mail headers, subject lines, and the body of emails to ensure that the emails were sent by authentic companies [28, 29]. Nonetheless, giant Google might use advanced spam classifiers with the help of machine learning algorithms, but this is an evolution from the earlier methods. In reality, it has been over two decades since machine learning has become the center of spam detection [30].

1.4.2 INTRUSION DETECTION

Intrusion detection systems attempt to find the presence of malicious users, unauthorized access on computer networks based on profile behavior violation, and activity. These attacks are basically categorized into two types: misuse based and anomaly based. Misuse-based detection is performed on the basis of its resemblance to already known attacks (supervised manner), whereas anomaly-based detection is performed by constructing a normal network or user behavior using frequent episode rules (FER) or association rules (AR), and looking for a deviation from the baseline behavior to determine whether to raise a flag or not. Anomaly-based detection does not use any pre-known attack database as it just detects suspicious behavior in an unsupervised manner [31, 32].

Machine learning-based misuse intrusion detection was initiated by DARPA to avoid the presence of humans in generating "specific list of rules to trigger an alert in presence of an attack." The researchers at DARPA fed network traffic profiles to ML classifiers to learn "how to identify previously seen attacks." The results concluded that machine learning can be a more competent in misuse-based detection [33]. Anomaly detection systems use unsupervised learning methods to "cluster" normal traffic within a network and a flag is raised when an activity deviates from the network pattern. These systems can normally detect "novel attacks," and the challenging task in such systems is defining or determining "baseline for normal traffic" since normal network traffic will never be constant. Thus, poorly designed anomaly detection systems might result in high false positives. In addition, such systems are very effective in securing individual machine or user behavior and may not produce expected results when implemented across a network [34].

The COVID-19 situation has forced organizations to come up with new approaches as their standard of operations and procedures have changed dramatically. This forces the organization to draw a new baseline, a lesson that many organizations learned as millions of employees started working from home in response to COVID-19 [35].

1.4.3 MALWARE DETECTION

Malware detection is a method of detecting files that are under virus attack by using specific indicators of compromise such as signatures (specific sequence of bytes or strings) on a system file. Malware defensive products such as antivirus maintain a "long list of malware signatures and also performs regular scans" to determine if any system or network file is associated with these "known definitions." Such traditional methods failed to capture "polymorphic or metamorphic viruses," which changes their own code each time so as the signatures [36]. In 2018, 94% of malware employed polymorphic traits. Traditional detections were found effective in identifying such polymorphic malware, but they proved to be more complex and computationally intensive as the attacker's skills keep on improving [37].

In 1996, IBM employed machine learning in detecting "boot sector viruses" [38]. In early 2000, statistical models and ML classifiers were used to detect malware, and these evaluations made a way for deep learning algorithms to extract "relevant features from raw data without human intervention or guidance" [39]. In the recent years, cyber defenders have been utilizing "sandboxes" to determine whether a file is malicious or not. Augmenting machine learning with sandboxes might not result in the same behavior while detecting malware [40].

1.5   DEEP LEARNING SECURITY AND PRIVACY CHALLENGES

Deep learning method's role in delivering privacy- and security-related services across various industries has become a hot topic in recent years as the business, governmental, and individual users believe that deep learning will protect their physical and logical resources from attackers with less damage or access. A very few studies have aimed to analyze these issues such as adversarial attacks and defenses in computer vision [41], privacy preserving techniques in DL [42], overall adversarial attacks and defense survey [43], and common security threats and defenses in ML [44], yet not all deep learning models were discussed in these studies.

In deep learning, an attack could either take place during the training or testing phase of a network model. A deep learning network under attack would result in false predictions as an attacker injects wrong samples (white-box attacks), whereas black box attacks cause the system to make fake predictions. Hence, an attack in deep learning exploits the predictive confidence of the system by not letting it collect the structure and parameters of the system (Figure 1.6).

Data injection results in training a bad model when poisoning samples are injected by the adversary as it has no knowledge of the training model and training data, and data modification pollutes the training data by imposing changes in the training data before training a target model. Logic corruption is tricky and difficult to defend as the adversary is aware of the target model and holds complete knowledge about it, thus being able to modify the learning algorithm at will [41, 43]. Hence, the adversary chooses an attack on their own such as using reverse engineering, shadow training models, and encoding the stolen information into models. For example, commercial APIs of Google, Microsoft, and so on charge customers for using their APIs with high protection as revealing their model could lead to a decline in their revenue. To summarize, an attack will either duplicate or modify the model or its parameters, which could result in designing or training a bad model, thus affecting the predictive results [45] (Figure 1.7).

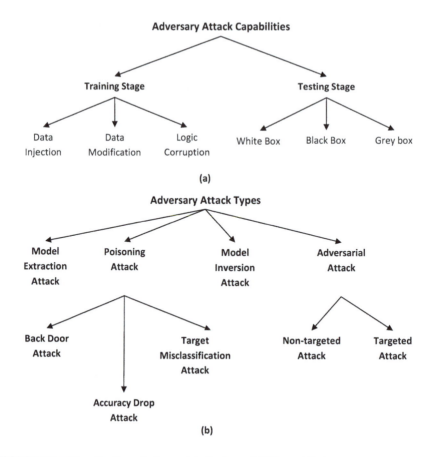

(a)

(b)

FIGURE 1.6   Classification of adversarial attack capabilities and its types.

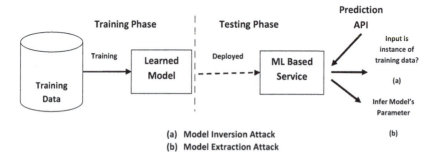

FIGURE 1.7   An illustration scenario of model inversion and model extraction attacks.

1.5.1 MODEL EXTRACTION ATTACK

This attack employs black-box access to duplicate the original AI model where the output function "f" is a replica of an input function "f' ", and a shadow training model [46] can extract near-perfect target ML models, which includes "logistic regression, decision trees, and neural networks by using equation solving, path finding, etc. [47]." Whereas studies such as [48] built meta-models to extract more information about the neural network architecture, [49] built an attack to steal more hyper-parameters from the neural network training set and model that determines the "balance between the loss function and regularization term in objective function" and [50] investigated on memory and timing side-channels attacks on convolutional neural networks (CNN).

1.5.2 MODEL INVERSION ATTACK

This attack is a type of feature estimation attack that aims to

> estimate certain features or statistical properties of the training data set used widely in white-box access, but also used in black-box with less effectiveness. In general, these type of attacks are targeted on learning sensitive genomic information of individuals by constructing a complete target vector with possible values (uses weighted probability estimate to check that the estimated value is correct one or not).
>
> [50]

A model inversion attack uses "reverse engineering" to adjust weight and obtain required values, and to be lethal when generative adversarial networks (GAN) are adopted, such as in facial recognition. This attack can both reconstruct the original image and also does deblurring of an original image. This attack is efficient in revealing more genomic private information about an individual [50, 51].

1.5.3 ADVERSARIAL ATTACK

This attack utilizes knowledge about the target model and crafts an adversarial model by adding imperceptible noise that motivates the classifier to make wrong predictions, and such a crafted model may also be effective in other models too, thus offering a "transferability" feature. A nontargeted adversarial attack is aimed at crafting adversarial examples for no particular class of a target model, whereas a target adversarial attack does this for a specific class of a target model [44].

1.5.4 POISONING ATTACK

This attack happens at testing stage where the adversary poisons the training data, which forces the learner to train a bad classifier, such as injecting malicious samples, modifying data labels, and causing corruption in the training data. An accuracy drop attack aims to reduce the performance of the target model; a target misclassification attack aims to misclassify the samples; and a backdoor attack aims to modify the input and forces the target model to produce output for that particular input [52].

1.6   OTHER ATTACKS

1.6.1   MEMBERSHIP INFERENCE ATTACK

This attack acquires knowledge to validate or determine whether the data record belongs to the model training data set or not, and it considers overfitting the structure and type of model as main factors to impose attack on vulnerable models [53]. The shadow model technique is widely used for such an attack. In addition, unsupervised binary classification [54] is used where no prior knowledge of a model or data distribution is required.

1.6.2   MODEL MEMORIZATION ATTACK

This attack targets to extract or recover exact values in individual samples without observing the training of a model, but is able to access the resulting model to steal sensitive information or parameters, which typically takes place during "model serving." To impose such a type of attack, an adversary uses various encoding techniques to steal sensitive information, such as LSB encoding, correlated value encoding, and sign encoding. This is the most generous attack and very effective to capture or extract more sensitive information about the training data than other available attacks [55].

1.7   DEEP LEARNING DEFENSES

There have been enormous research studies done on defensive mechanisms to protect the target model in both training and testing phases from adversaries to ensure security and privacy properties of community-based and individual sensitive information. A community-based information-sharing scheme was introduced in [56] where a clustering-based privacy attack was prevented as this scheme changes the "entire spatial and temporal features of a model". Deep learning-based techniques are effective in defining "well designed inputs called 'adversarial examples'" in [57]. The fast gradient sign method (FGSM) was introduced to generate examples that can fool both human and computer like [58]. The linear nature of neural networks makes them more vulnerable to adversarial examples (Figure 1.8).

Differential privacy aims to "guarantee an algorithm to learn statistical information about the population without disclosing sensitive information about individuals".

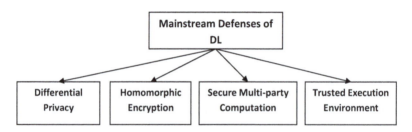

FIGURE 1.8   Mainstream defenses against DL attacks.

Gaussian distribution or Laplace distribution are used to generate noise samples that prevent an adversary from inferring information about the data set. This approach is classified into three categories on the basis of where the noise is added: gradient perturbation, objective perturbation, and label perturbation [59]. Homomorphic encryption (HE) offers protection through encryption and decryption since neural networks involve "large number of additions and multiplications," and this approach works effectively in both partial and full forms as well. It is evident [60] that partial homomorphic encryption (PHE) with additive operations is effective and best suitable for deep learning's complex computation. Fully homomorphic encryption (FHE) supports all sets of operations on encrypted data and lattice-based cryptography. Although FHE supports all operations on cipher text on encryption, it has limited support (integer-type data and computational complexity) when applied to a deep learning model. There still exist a lot of custom works for every deep learning model to enhance its performance with an FHE environment and the efficiency of computation [61, 62].

Secure multi-party computation (SMC) addresses the problem of "joint computing to maintain participant's data privacy in a flock of the non-trusted participant" by keeping the participants from knowing the data of each other to preserve privacy [63]. SMC has two operating scenarios: in the first scenario, the data holders do not expose all the data to a single server to train the model; instead, the data holder distributes the data among multiple servers to maintain privacy. In such a situation, each server does not know nor understand what happens on other servers. In the second scenario, multiple data holders jointly train the deep learning model using "aggregate training method" to preserve the privacy of training data.

In [64], collaborative deep learning was introduced to share inputs for joint learning without sacrificing both privacy and accuracy; however, [65] claimed that a small portion of gradients (stored on cloud servers) might increase the risk of letting e adversaries extract the local data features; hence, the work has added flavour homomorphic encryption and considered "honest but curious server." However, this approach had

---

TABLE 1.2A
Summary of Applications for (a) Prevention (b) Detection (c) Response and Recovery and (d) Active Defense

Security task	Underlying Technology	Task Significance	Transformative Potential
Fuzzing	Deep Learning	High	Medium-High
Pentesting	Reinforcement Learning	High	Medium-High
Bug Triage and Classification	Natural Language Processing, traditional ML Methods	Medium	Medium
Vulnerability Severity Assessment	Natural Language Processing, traditional ML Methods	Medium	Medium-Low

TABLE 1.2B
Summary of Applications for Detection of (c) Response and Recovery and (d) Active Defense

Security Task	Underlying Technology	Task Significance	Transformative Potential
Accurate Detection	Deep learning	High	Low
Alert Prioritization	Deep Learning	Medium-High	Medium
Adversarial Hardening of Detection Systems	Generative Adversarial Networks (GANS)	Medium-High	Medium-Low

TABLE 1.2C
Summary of Applications for Response and Recovery and (d) Active Defense

Security Task	Underlying Technology	Task Significance	Transformative Potential
Adversary Engagement	Reinforcement Learning	High	Medium-Low
Moving Target Defense	Reinforcement Learning	High	Medium-High

TABLE 1.2D
Summary of Applications for Active Defense

Security Task	Underlying Technology	Task Significance	Transformative Potential
Deceptive Document Generation	NLP, GANs	Medium-Low	High
Dynamic Honeypotting	Reinforcement Learning	Medium	Medium-High
Automated Phishing Response	NLP, Reinforcement Learning	Low	Medium-High
Dark Web Threat Intelligence	NLP	Medium	Medium
Attack Clustering for Attribution	NLP, Traditional ML Methods	Medium-Low	Medium
Code De-Anonymization	NLP	Low	Medium-Low

led to increased communication overhead among the cloud server and the learning participants. In [66], privacy preserving was achieved through "multiparty computation setting with OT, secret sharing, and Yao's Garbled Circuits protocol, which yielded better protection when implemented in simple neural networks".

1.7.1 TRUSTED EXECUTION ENVIRONMENT

A trusted execution environment (TEE) offers an independent execution environment for authorized and trusted applications to ensure the integrity and confidentiality of the data, codes, and model with access control mechanisms while operating on an untrusted platform [67]. In [68], Software Guard Extensions (SGX) was used to protect memory regions (enclaves) where the encrypted training data and training model are executed (encryption and decryption) after verification. In [69], Chiron was used for joint collaboration on a machine learning-based application as a service cloud platform. Following this, Ryoan sandbox was introduced to provide a distributed sandbox by "leveraging enclaves." Although, Chiron is efficient as it employs multiple enclaves during training and testing, only the data owner can query a training model. Thus, Chiron is not appropriate in a distributed environment.

In [70], a deepen community was introduced to "partition a given neural network into FrontNet and BackNet," where FrontNet is located in a trusted environment and BackNet is in an untrusted environment (SGX). In [71], a Slalom framework was proposed, which employs Freivalds's algorithm to achieve and verify the linear operator's correctness. In this framework, a precalculated blinding factor was considered and the DNN execution part was outsourced from TEE to a co-located, untrusted device such as a GPU. In [72], MLCapsule was proposed, which was protected by TEE in which ML algorithms were executed in offline deployed clients. This framework uses transparent protocol, and the data are stored locally, and an ML model is calculated by the enclave in TEE. Enclaves play an important role in both encryption and decryption. MLCapsule supports large-scale network encapsulation and also integrates advance defense mechanisms against deep learning attacks with low computational cost.

1.8 RANSOMWARE AND EXTORTION RANSOMWARE ATTACKS

Ransomware is

> malware that employs encryption to hold victim's information at ransom. It prevents the authorized individual user or organization from accessing their files, databases, or applications. A ransom aims to paralyze an entire business firm's functionalities by targeting or attacking its databases and file servers, after which a ransom is demanded for releasing those resources for access.
> www.trellix.com/en-us/security-awareness/ransomware/what-is-ransomware.html#:~:text=Ransomware%20is%20malware%20that%20employs,then%20demanded%20to%20provide%20access

From statistical reports, it is evident that cybercriminals target critical industries in the business market such as oil and gas, food and beverages, transport, healthcare, and finance. The end goals of these attacks are to create maximum disruption by launching crippling attacks on network system resources. These kinds of attacks cause damage and also lead to unnecessary expenses for both businesses and governmental organizations as the cybercriminals generate "billions of dollars" in payments [73]. A Blackfog [74] blog article warned that the number of ransomware attacks would reach $6 trillion in the year 2021 ($3 trillion in 2020), and some newer forms of attack would be more sophisticated and disruptive (Figures 1.9 and 1.10).

A *Computer Weekly* [75] report stated that attackers not only employ a "triple extortion" ransomware technique that steals sensitive information from customers, business vendors, or firms, but also threaten to disclose stolen information publicly

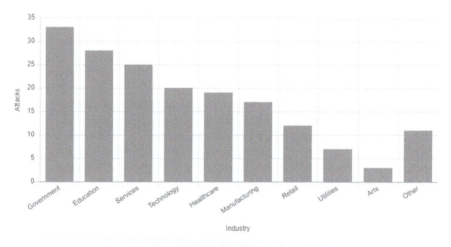

FIGURE 1.9   Ransomware attacks by Industry [2].

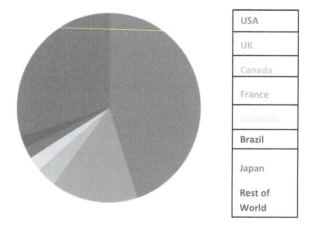

FIGURE 1.10   Ransomware attacks by country [2].

unless a demanded payment is made. Business firms in the Europe, Middle East, and Africa (EMEA) region have experienced a 36% increase in such attacks and 24% in America. For the past two years, the attackers have considered ransomware (extortion) a highly lucrative business to make billions or trillions with the use of penetration tools like Cobalt Strike or Bloodhound that permit "live access for the hackers on compromised network infrastructures on the fly." In spite of increased attention and investments made from governments and law enforcement agencies, ransomware attacks continue to penetrate giant businesses like Solarwinds, Colonial Pipeline, JBS, and Kayesa. Extortion ransomware attacks are the most dangerous of all as they can affect multiple organizations at once and firms must establish "collateral damage strategies" to tackle such attacks [74, 75].

Cybercriminals use anonymous tools like the dark web and the deep web to inject ransomware attacks into a targeted database and file servers. The deep web represents the 90% of the Internet, which consists of a "large array of private databases and information compiled by governments, universities, corporations and other private institutions" and is not indexed by search engines like Google. The dark web uses only 6% of the Internet where illegal trade takes place among cybercriminals such as "purchasing stolen credit card numbers, drugs and firearms." The deep web does not require any specific software or browser to consume content-specific data from a network or clients, whereas the dark web uses anonymous browsers, such as The Onion Router (TOR), to access the target content from the network or server [76].

The Onion Router is an anonymous web browser that employs anonymous route changes like a series of relay stations to access and forward the content without making a direct connection. It is a legal browser, widely used by the journalists and law enforcement authorities to conduct private communication or transactions (purchasing bitcoins). Unfortunately, TOR is also used by the cybercriminals to abstract their activities and remain undetected [77].

1.9 CONCLUSION

Deep learning algorithms have become an integral part of all business industries in recent years, such as supply chain, medical image processing, computer vision, and more, but the security industry has not yet have utilized this technique effectively as some experts believe that embedding deep learning mechanisms might be complex and computational cost will be significantly high. Still, business giants like Google, Apple, and other large companies have been successful in implementing deep learning techniques such as natural language processing and deep-reinforcement learning into their applications. Moreover, researchers interested in developing deep learning algorithms to offer enhanced privacy and security for government, business, and individuals have become greatly concerned with this issue in recent years. The number of ransomware attacks on various business industries across countries became increasingly high in 2020 and 2021. Therefore, there still exists an engineering need to study, understand, and develop more advanced and improved deep learning algorithms, which are vital. This chapter briefly discussed the importance of machine learning and deep learning algorithms, various adversary attacks, and defensive mechanisms used in deep learning. Finally, this chapter summarized the recent ransomware attacks on various industries and their impact on those industries.

TABLE 1.3
Summary of Important Ransomware Attacks on Various Industries (January–August 2021)

Month and Year	Company Name	Location	Nature of Business/ Products/ Services	Impact of Attack	Ransomware used
January 2021	Apex Laboratory	New York, USA	Provides Medical Testing Services	Personnel and heath information of some patients in its environment were encrypted and inaccessible	DoppelPaymer ransomware
	Amey	United Kingdom	Infrastructure support service	Documents and correspondence to government departments were stolen	Mount Locker ransomware
	Hackney Council	London, UK	Local government authority in London Borough of Hackney	Personally identifiable information was leaked	PSYA ransomware (double extortion attack)
	Dassault Falcon Jet Corp	USA	Subsidiary of Dassault Aviation	Attackers had access to the systems for six months and stole employees' personal information	Ragnar Locker Gang
February 2021	**Foxtons Group**	United Kingdom	A British estate agents	Large quantity of personnel and financial information of customers was listed on The Dark Web. 16,000 credit card details were present.	**Egregor Group**
	Ness Digital Engineering Company	Israel	Israel-based U.S. IT provider that offers various IT related services in India, the U.S., and Israel.	Most of the system files were encrypted and inaccessible	Ragnar Locker
	CD Projekt	Poland	A video game company	Accessed the network illegally and encrypted some devices	HelloKitty ransomware

Date	Organization	Location	Description	Details	Ransomware/Group
	Dax-Cote d'Argent Hospital Center	France	Provides hospitality and healthcare services	Reading a medical file to a catering system had been affected and the hospital was forced to accept only major emergencies	Egregor ransomware / Darkside ransomware
	Discount Car and Truck Rental	Canada	A car and truck rental agency that is part of Enterprise Group	Attackers had stolen corporate, banking, and franchise data of 120 GB	
March 2021	Stanley Systems	Oklahoma, USA	Managed service provides for its clients of different businesses	Attackers obtained sensitive data that which included clients' personnel data such as passport details, medical documents, etc., along with 1,000 Social Security numbers	REvil ransomware
	Qualys	California, USA	Provides cloud-based security and lower-cost operations for business organizations	Attackers had stolen invoices, tax documents, and purchase orders	Clop ransomware
	Acer	–	Computing devices and peripherals manufacturing services	Attackers stole information such as bank balances, balance spreadsheets, and bank communications	REvil ransomware ($50 million ransom)
	CNA	USA	US-based insurance giant	Affected 15,000 devices on its network and employees who remotely logged in using virtual private networks (VPN)	Evil Corp Hacking Group
	University of Maryland	Maryland, USA	Offers academic courses and research opportunities for the students	Sensitive information of the students such as photos, Social Security numbers, home addresses, immigration status, and more	Clop ransomware

(continued)

TABLE 1.3 (Continued)
Summary of Important Ransomware Attacks on Various Industries (January–August 2021)

Month and Year	Company Name	Location	Nature of Business/ Products/ Services	Impact of Attack	Ransomware used
April 2021	Asteelflash	France	Electronics manufacturing services company	Sensitive information had been stolen	REvil Gang ransomware ($24 million)
	Broward County School District	Florida, USA	Offers education and related services, courses to students	Sensitive information of both students and teachers was stolen	Conti ransomware gang ($40 million)
	Home Hardware	Canada	Hardware dealer and retailer	Corporate data was stolen	Darkside ransomware group
	PierreFabre	France	A leading pharmaceutical company	Production was halted due to ransomware attack	REvil ransomware group ($50 million)
	The University of Portsmouth	United Kingdom	Offers academic and research courses to students across the globe	Attackers forced a "technical disruption" to its IT network infrastructure	Attacker is unknown and incident is being investigated
May 2021	Volue Technology	Norway	Leading supplier of technology services. The firm included its chief executive's telephone number and email address, and updates related to the attacks.	Attackers gained access to the databases	RYUK ransomware
	Colonial Pipeline	USA	Largest fuel pipeline industry that supplies gas to several states of USA	The attack caused shortage of gas as it created havoc	The DarkSide ($5 million)

	Organization	Location	Description	Impact	Attacker
	Yamabiko	Tokyo, Japan	Manufactures power tools, agricultural and industrial machinery	Attackers exfiltrated 0.5 TB data from the company's database	Babuk ransomware gang
	Brenntag	Germany	Chemical distribution company	Attackers encrypted 150 GB data during the attack	The DarkSide ransomware ($4.4 million paid in bitcoin)
	Azusa Police Department	Southern California, USA	Government department that offers various services to public	Cybercriminals posted 7GB of data on the Dark Web that consists of 48,000 residents' medical information, driver's license numbers, financial information, and more	The DoppelPaymer
June 2021	ADATA	Taiwan	Manufactures computer memory and storage components	1.5 TB of confident data was stolen from the database and file servers	The Ragnar Locker REvil ransomware Gang
	Sol Oriens	USA	Manages nuclear weapons programs for National Nuclear Security Administration	Sol Oriens claimed that no data was compromised during the attack	The Criminal Gang
	The Town of Freeport	Maine, USA	Shipping-related business services	Entire network was shut down and no data breach reported by the data	The Criminal Gang
	Mountain Regional	Summit Country	Water district provides to the public	Some of the hardware resources encrypted by the cybercriminals	

(continued)

TABLE 1.3 (Continued)
Summary of Important Ransomware Attacks on Various Industries (January–August 2021)

Month and Year	Company Name	Location	Nature of Business/ Products/ Services	Impact of Attack	Ransomware used
July 2021	Coop	Sweden	A chain of supermarkets that offers everyday products to its customers	Colossal cyber attack forced the company to close half of its outlets (around 400) across the country	The REvil Gang
	SYNNEX	California, USA	Technology distributor through its supply chains	Company databases and Microsoft accounts had been attacked by the cyber criminal	Cozy Bear
	Leonardtown Maryland	Maryland, USA	A government authority in Leonardtown	Kaseya ransomware attack was injected into its IT management company JustTech. The authorities could not open documents and their computers froze following a pop-up message regarding the attack	The REvil Gang ($45,000 per computer demanded)
	Guess	USA	U.S.-based fashion brand and retailer across various continents such as Europe, Asia, etc.	200GB of personnel data was accessed by the attackers to create a consumer data breach	The DarkSide ransomware Gang
	Morgan County Schools	Tennessee, USA	Offers academic and practical courses to students	Attackers targeted school's computers and accessed office-related information.	The REvil Gang

REFERENCES

1. Imamverdiyev, Y. N., & Abdullayeva, F. J. (2018). Deep Learning method for Denial of Service Attack Detection based on restricted Boltzmann machine. *Big Data 6*(2), 159–169. https://doi:10.1089/big.2018.0023.
2. Lin, T. C. (2016). Financial weapons of war. *Minnesota Law Review 102*(3), 1377–1440.
3. Cyberspace Policy Review. (2009). *Assuring a Trusted and Resilient Information and Communications Infrastructure*. Executive Office of the President of the United States.
4. Musser, Micah, & Garriott, Ashton. (2021). Machine learning and cybersecurity: Hype and reality. Center for Security and Emerging Technology (CSET). June. https://doi.org/10.51593/2020CA004.
5. Wang, W., Zhu, M., Zeng, X., Ye, X., & Sheng, Y. (2017). Malware traffic classification using convolutional neural network for representation learning. In: *Proceedings of the International Conference on Information Networking*, 712–717. Academic Press.
6. Wang, Z. (2015). *The applications of deep learning on traffic identification*. Blackhat.
7. Tang, T. A., Mhamdi, L., McLernon, D., Zaidi, S. A., & Ghogho, M. (2016). Deep learning approach for network intrusion detection in software defined networking. In: *Proceedings of the IEEE International Conference on Wireless Networks and Mobile Communications*, 258–263. IEEE Press. https://doi.org/10.1109/WINCOM.2016.7777224.
8. Brownlee, Jason. (2019). What is deep learning? Machine Learning Mastery. Updated August 2020. Available at: https://machinelearningmastery.com/what-is-deep-learning/. Accessed: July 2021.
9. Bengio, Yoshua. (2012). Deep learning of representations for unsupervised and transfer learning. Workshop on Unsupervised and Transfer Learning. *JMLR: Workshop and Conference Proceedings 27*: 17–37.
10. Delua, Julianna. (2021). Supervised vs. unsupervised learning: What's the difference? Artificial Intelligence, 12 March. Available at: www.ibm.com/cloud/blog/supervised-vs-unsupervised-learning. Accessed: July 2021.
11. Goodfellow, I., Pouget-Abadie, J., Mirza, M., Hu, B., Warde-Farley, D., Ozair, S., & Bengio, Y. (2014). Generative adversarial nets. In: Z. Ghahramani (ed.), *Proceedings of the 27th International Conference on Neural Information Processing Systems*, vol. 2, 2672–2680. MIT Press.
12. Bansal, Shubham. (2021). Supervised and unsupervised learning. GeeksforGeeks, updated March 22, 2021. Available at: www.geeksforgeeks.org/supervised-unsupervised-learning/. Accessed: July 2021.
13. Osinski, Blazej, & Budek, Konrad. (2018). What is reinforcement learning? The complete guide. deepsense.ai, July 5. Available at: https://deepsense.ai/what-is-reinforcement-learning-the-complete-guide/. Accessed: August 24, 2021.
14. Nguyen, Thanh Thi, & Reddi, Vijay Janapa. (2019). Deep reinforcement learning for cyber security. *arXiv*: 1906.05700 [cs.CR]. Available at: https://arxiv.org/pdf/1906.05799.pdf.
15. Elderman, Richard et al. (2017). Adversarial reinforcement learning in a cyber security simulation. *ICAART*. Available at: www.ai.rug.nl/~mwiering/GROUP/ARTICLES/CyberSec_ICAART.pdf.
16. Bhatt, Shweta. (2018). Reinforcement Learning 101: Learn the essentials of Reinforcement Learning. towards data science, March 19. Available at: https://towardsdatascience.com/reinforcement-learning-101-e24b50e1d292. Accessed: August 24, 2021.

17. Thillaiarasu N., Gowthaman N., & Chenthur Pandian S. (2022). Design of a confidentiality model using semantic-based information segmentation (SBIS) and scattered storage in cloud computing. In: Nath Sur, S., Balas, V. E., Bhoi, A.K., & Nayyar, A. (eds.), *IoT and IoE Driven Smart Cities*, 183–213. EAI/Springer Innovations in Communication and Computing. Springer. https://doi.org/10.1007/978-3-030-82715-1_9.

18. Malini P., Gowthaman N., Gautami A., & Thillaiarasu N. (2022). Internet of Everything (IoE) in smart city paradigm using advanced sensors for handheld devices and equipment. In: Nath Sur, S., Balas, V. E., Bhoi, A. K., and Nayyar, A. (eds.), *IoT and IoE Driven Smart Cities*, 121–141. EAI/Springer Innovations in Communication and Computing. Springer. https://doi.org/10.1007/978-3-030-82715-1_6

19. Thillaiarasu N., Pandian S. C., & Gowthaman N. (2022). Novel heuristic scheme to enforce safety and confidentiality using feature-based encryption in multi-cloud environment (MCE). In: Guarda, T., Anwar, S., Leon, M., & Mota Pinto, F. J. (eds.), 441–456. *Information and Knowledge in Internet of Things*. EAI/Springer Innovations in Communication and Computing. Springer. https://doi.org/10.1007/978-3-030-75123-4_20

20. Preethi, P., Asokan, R., Thillaiarasu, N., & Saravanan, T. (2021). An effective digit recognition model using enhanced convolutional neural network based chaotic grey wolf optimization. *Journal of Intelligent and Fuzzy Systems* 41(2): 3727–3737.

21. Thillaiarasu, N., Pandian, S.C., Vijayakumar, V. et al. (2021). Designing a trivial information relaying scheme for assuring safety in mobile cloud computing environment. *Wireless Networks* 27: 5477–5490. https://doi.org/10.1007/s11276-019-02113-4

22. Thillaiarasu, N., & Chenthur Pandian, S. (2019). A novel scheme for safeguarding confidentiality in public clouds for service users of cloud computing. *Cluster Computing* 22: 1179–1188. https://doi.org/10.1007/s10586-017-1178-8

23. Shyamambika, N., & Thillaiarasu, N. (2016). A survey on acquiring integrity of shared data with effective user termination in the cloud. In: *10th International Conference on Intelligent Systems and Control (ISCO)*, 1–5. IEE Explore. https://doi.org/10.1109/ISCO.2016.7726893.

24. Thillaiarasu, N., & Chenthur Pandian, S. (2016). Enforcing security and privacy over multi-cloud framework using assessment techniques. *10th International Conference on Intelligent Systems and Control (ISCO)*, 1–5. IEE Explore. https://doi.org/10.1109/ISCO.2016.7727001.

25. Shyamambika, N., & Thillaiarasu, N. (2016). Attaining integrity, secured data sharing and removal of misbehaving client in the public cloud using an external agent and secure encryption technique. *Advances in Natural and Applied Sciences* 10(9 SE): 421–432.

26. Singh, Satnam, & Balamurali, A. R. (2018). Using the power of deep learning for cyber security. Analytics Vidhya, July 5. Available at: www.analyticsvidhya.com/blog/2018/07/using-power-deep-learning-cyber-security/. Accessed: August 2021.

27. Lamont, Jonathan. (2019). Google uses machine learning to catch spam missed by Gmail filters. MobileSyrup, February. Available at: https://mobilesyrup.com/2019/02/06/google-machine-learning-gmail-spam-filter/. Accessed: August 2021.

28. Hu W., Liao Y., & Vemuri V.R. (2003). Robust anomaly detection using support vector machines. In: *Proceedings of the International Conference on Machine Learning*, 282–289. CiteSeer.

29. Heller, K. A., Svore, M., Keromytis, A. D., & Stolfo, S. J. (2003). One class support vector machines for detecting anomalous Windows registry accesses. In: *Proceedings of the Workshop on Data Mining for Computer Security*. IEEE. 1–8. https://citeserx.ist.psu.edu/viewdoc/similar;jsessionid=948C653252FA5398263B7043511A4EE4?doi=10.1.1.10.7512&type=sc

30. Buchanan, Ben. (2020). *The hacker and the state: Cyber attacks and the new normal of geopolitics*. Harvard University Press.
31. Sobers, Rob. (2017). 110 Must-Know134 Cybersecurity Statistics and Trends for 20210. Inside Out Security blog. Varonis. Accessed: June 25, 2021. Available at: www.varonis.com/blog/cybersecurity-statistics/.
32. Casey, Tami. (2018). Survey: 27 percent of IT professionals receive more than 1 million security alerts daily. imperva, May 28. Available at: www.imperva.com/blog/27-percent-of-it-professionals-receive-morethan-1-million-security-alerts-daily/.
33. For a competing view, see David Brumley. (2019). Why I'm not sold on machine learning in autonomous security. CSO Online, August 27. Available at: www.csoonline.com/article/3434081/why-im-not-sold-onmachine-learning-in-autonomous-security.html.
34. Lippmann, Richard et al. (2000). The 1999 DARPA off-line intrusion detection evaluation. *Computer Networks* 34(4) (October 1): 579–595.
35. Palmieri, Francesco, Fiore, Ugo, & Castiglione, Aniello. (2014). A distributed approach to network anomaly detection based on independent component analysis. *Concurrency and Computation: Practice & Experience* 26(5): 1113–1129.
36. Verbeke, Stephen (2020). COVID-19's impact on cybersecurity incident response. Novetta, May 26. Available at: www.novetta.com/2020/05/cyber-covid/.
37. Irshad, Mustafa et al. (2018). Effective methods to detect metamorphic malware: A systematic review. *International Journal of Electronic Security and Digital Forensics* 10(2): 138–154.
38. Duran, Nicholas et al. (2018). 2018 Webroot threat report. Webroot. Available at: www-cdn.webroot. com/9315/2354/6488/2018-Webroot-Threat-Report_US-ONLINE.pdf.
39. Tesauro, G. J., Kephart, J. O., & Sorkin, G. B. (1996). Neural networks for computer virus recognition. *IEEE Expert* 11(4): 5–6.
40. Gibert, Daniel, Mateu, Carles, & Planes, Jordi. (2020). The rise of machine learning for detection and classification of malware: Research developments, trends and challenges. *Journal of Network and Computer Applications* 153 (March). https://doi.org/10.1016/j.jnca.2019.102526.
41. Darshan, S. L. S., Kumara, M. A. A., & Jaidhar, C. D. (2016). Windows malware detection based on Cuckoo Sandbox generated report using machine learning algorithm. In: *11th International Conference on Industrial and Information Systems (ICIIS)*, 534–539. IEEE.
42. Akhtar, N., & Mian, A. (2018). Threat of adversarial attacks on deep learning in computer vision: A survey. *IEEE Access*, 6: 14410–14430.
43. Boulemtafes, A., Derhab, A., & Challal, Y. (2020). A review of privacy preserving techniques for deep learning. *Neurocomputing*, 384: 21–45.
44. Yuan, X. , He, P., Zhu, Q., and Li, X. (2019). Adversarial examples: Attacks and defenses for deep learning. *IEEE Transactions on Neural Networks and Learning Systems*, 30(9): 2805–2824.
45. Liu, Q., Li, P., Zhao, W., Cai, W., Yu, S., & Leung, V.C.M. (2018). A survey on security threats and defensive techniques of machine learning: A data driven view. *IEEE Access*, 6: 12103–12117.
46. Liu, Bo, Ding, Ming, Shaham, Sina, Rahayu, Wenny, Farokhi, F., & Lin, Z. (2020). When machine learning meets privacy: A survey and outlook. *ACM Computing Surveys*, 1(1). https://doi.org/10.1145/nnnnnnn.nnnnnnn.
47. Tramèr, Florian, Zhang, Fan, Juels, Ari, Reiter, Michael K., & Ristenpart, Thomas. (2016). Stealing machine learning models via prediction APIs. In: Holz, Thorsten

(ed.), *SEC'16: Proceedings of the 25th USENIX Security Symposiu*m, 601–618. USENIX Association.

48. Lowd, Daniel, & Meek, Christopher. (2005). Adversarial learning. In: *KDD'05: Proceedings of the ACM International Conference on Knowledge Discovery and Data Mining*, 641–647. ACM Digital Library. https://doi.org/10.1145/1081 870.1081950.

49. Joon Oh, Seong, Schiele, Bernt, & Fritz, Mario. (2019). Towards reverse-engineering black-box neural networks. In: Samek, Wojciech, Montavon, Grégoire, Vedaldi, Andrea, Hansen, Lars Kai, & Müller, Klaus-Robert (eds.), *Explainable AI: Interpreting, Explaining and Visualizing Deep Learning*, 121–141. Springer Nature.

50. Wang, Binghui, & Zhenqiang Gong, Neil. (2018). Stealing hyperparameters in machine learning. In: *Proceedings of the IEEE Symposium on Security and Privacy (SP'18)*, 36–52. IEEE. https://doi.org/10.1109/SP.2018.00038.

51. Fredrikson, Matt, Jha, Somesh, & Ristenpart, Thomas. (2015). Model inversion attacks that exploit confidence information and basic countermeasures. In: *Proceedings of the ACM Conference on Computer and Communications Security (CCS'15)*. 1322–1333. ACM. https://doi.org/10.1145/2810103.2813677.

52. Ateniese, Giuseppe, Mancini, Luigi V., Spognardi, Angelo, Villani, Antonio, Vitali, Domenico, & Felici, Giovanni. 2015. Hacking smart machines with smarter ones: How to extract meaningful data from machine learning classifiers. *International Journal of Security and Networks* 10(3): 137–150. https://doi.org/ 10.1504/IJSN.2015.071829.

53. Melis, Luca, Song, Congzheng, De Cristofaro, Emiliano, & Shmatikov, Vitaly. (2019). Exploiting unintended feature leakage in collaborative learning. In: *Proceedings of the IEEE Symposium on Security and Privacy (SP'19)*, 691–706. IEEE.

54. Salem, Ahmed, Zhang, Yang, Humbert, Mathias, Berrang, Pascal, Fritz, Mario, & Backes, Michael. (2019). ML-leaks: Model and data independent membership inference attacks and defenses on machine learning models. In: *Proceedings of Network and Distributed Systems Security Symposium (NDSS'19)*. https://doi.org/10.14722/ ndss.2019.23119.

55. Song, Congzheng, Ristenpart, Thomas, & Shmatikov, Vitaly. (2017). Machine learning models that remember too much. In: *Proceedings of the ACM Conference on Computer and Communications Security (CCS'17)*, 587–601. ACM. https://doi.org/ 10.1145/3133956.3134077.

56. Sanil, Ashish P., Karr, Alan F., Lin, Xiaodong, & Reiter, Jerome P. (2004). Privacy preserving regression modelling via distributed computation. In: *Proceedings of the ACM SIGKDD International Conference on Knowledge Discovery and Data Mining (KDD'04)*, 677–682. https://doi.org/10.1145/1014052.1014139.

57. Liu, Bo, Zhou, Wanlei, Yu, Shui , Wang, Kun, Wang, Yu, Xiang, Yong, & Li, Jin. (2017). Home location protection in mobile social networks: a community based method (short paper). In: *Proceedings of the International Conference on Information Security Practice and Experience (ISPEC'17)*, 694–704. Springer.

58. Goodfellow, Ian J., Pouget-Abadie, Jean, Mirza, Mehdi, Xu, Bing, David Warde-Farley, David, Ozair, Sherjil, Courville, Aaron, & Bengio, Yoshua. (2014). Generative adversarial nets. In: *Advances in Neural Information Processing Systems (NIPS'14)*, vol. 3: 2672–2680. NeurIPS Proceedings.

59. Poursaeed, Omid, Katsman, Isay, Gao, Bicheng, & Belongie, Serge. (2018). Generative adversarial perturbations. In: *Proceedings of the IEEE Computer Society Conference*

on Computer Vision and Pattern Recognition (CVPR'18), 4422–4431. https://doi.org/10.1109/CVPR.2018.00465.

60. Dwork, C. (2008). Differential privacy: A survey of results. In: *Proceedings of the International Conference on Theory and Applications of Models of Computation*, 1–19. Springer.

61. Paillier, P. (1999). Public-key cryptosystems based on composite degree residuosity classes. In: *Proceedings of the International Conference on Theory and Applications of Cryptographic Techniques*, 223–238. Springer.

62. Gentry, C. (2009). Fully homomorphic encryption using ideal lattices. In: *Proceedings of the 41st Annual ACM Symposium on Theory of Computing*, 169–178.

63. Liu, X., Deng, R. H., Choo, K.-K.-R., Yang, Y., & Pang, H. 2020. Privacy-preserving outsourced calculation toolkit in the cloud. *IEEE Transactions on Dependable and Secure Computing*, 17(5): 898–911.

64. Goldreich, O., Micali, S., & Wigderson, A. (2019). How to play any mental game, or a completeness theorem for protocols with honest majority. In: Goldreich, O. (ed.), *Providing Sound Foundations for Cryptography: On the Work of Shafi Goldwasser and Silvio Micali*, 307–328. ACM. https://doi.org/10.1145/3335741.3335755.

65. Shokri, R., & Shmatikov, V. (2015). Privacy-preserving deep learning. In: *Proceedings of the 53rd Annual Allerton Conference on Communication, Control, and Computing (Allerton)*, 1310–1321. IEEE Press.

66. Phong, L. T., Aono, Y., Hayashi, T., Wang, L., & Moriai, S. (2018). Privacy-preserving deep learning via additively homomorphic encryption. *IEEE Transactions on Information Forensics and Security*, 13(5): 1333–1345.

67. Mohassel, P., & Zhang, Y. (2017). Secure ML: A system for scalable privacy-preserving machine learning. In: *Proceedings IEEE Symposium on Security and Privacy (SP)*, 19–38. IEEE.

68. Liu, X., Deng, R. H. , Wu, P., & Yang, Y. 2020. Lightning-fast and privacy-preserving outsourced computation in the cloud. *Cybersecurity* 3(1): 1–21.

69. Hunt, T., Song, C., Shokri, R., Shmatikov, V., & Witchel, E. (2018). Chiron: Privacy-preserving machine learning as a service. *arXiv*:1803.05961. Available at: https://arxiv.org/abs/1803.05961.

70. Hunt, T., Zhu, Z., Xu, Y., Peter, S., & Witchel, E. (2018). Ryoan: A distributed sandbox for untrusted computation on secret data. *ACM Transactions on Computer Systems* 35(4): 1–32.

71. Gu, Z., Huang, H., Zhang, J., Su, D., Lamba, A., Pendarakis, D., & Molloy, I. (2018). Securing input data of deep learning inference systems via partitioned enclave execution. *arXiv*:1807.00969. Available at: https://arxiv.org/abs/1807.00969.

72. Freivalds, R. (1977). Probabilistic machines can use less running time. In: *Proceedings of IFIP Congress*, 839: 842.

73. Hanzlik, L. et al. (2018). MLCapsule: Guarded offline deployment of machine learning as a service. *arXiv*:1808.00590. Available at: https://arxiv.org/abs/1808.00590.

74. What is ransomware? (2021). Trellix. Available at: www.mcafee.com/enterprise/en-in/security-awareness/ransomware.html. Accessed August 2021.

75. The state of ransomware. (2021). Blackfog, August 2. Available at: www.blackfog.com/the-state-of-ransomware-in-2021/#Ransomware_Attacks_by_Industry. Accessed August 2021.

76. Klovig Skelton, Sebastian. (2021). Ransomware attacks increase dramatically during 2021. *ComputerWeekly*, August 3. Available at: www.computerweekly.com/news/252504676/Ransomware-attacks-increase-dramatically-during-2021. Accessed August 2021.

77. Anonymous ransomware attack tools. (2021). Blackfog, June. Available at: www. blackfog.com/anonymous-ransomware-attack-tools/. Accessed August 2021.

78. Laurent, Maryline, & Levallois-Barth, Claire. (2015). Privacy management and protection of personal data. In: Laurent, Maryline, & Bouzefrane, Samia (eds.), *Digital Identity Management*, 137–205. Elsevier. https://doi.org/10.1016/ B978-1-78548-004-1.50004-3.

2 Crypto-Based Secure Outbound Supply Chain Authentication for Industry 4.0

M. Narayanan[1], T. Poongothai[1], and T. Saravanan[2]
[1]Department of Computer Science and Engineering, St. Martin's Engineering College, Secunderabad, India
[2]Department of CSE, Faculty of Engineering and Technology, JAIN (Deemed-to-be-university), Bengaluru, India

CONTENTS

2.1 INTRODUCTION

With the emergence of Industry 5.0 and other similar ideas being addressed more often, the Internet of Things (IoT) has recently been represented as a significant notion in helping technology summarise concepts in a real-time context. It not only links devices but also incorporates the internet, allowing for a variety of product production services [1,2]. Privacy-preserving mechanisms with cloud environments are commonly used to provide service provisioning (internet). With the importance of internet services, the interconnection of various gadgets works abruptly to dramatically increase productivity and efficiency. It is becoming a trending environment as IoT-enabled equipment across the administrative region interconnects to accomplish industrial operations, resulting in increased productivity and lower management costs. Furthermore, dealing with product manufacture on a stand-alone basis in a sophisticated manner is quite difficult. The stretching across domains with collaboration connection is linked to complicated production functionality. In these contexts, devices deployed across many domains must connect with one another in order to exchange information and improve cooperation.

Despite the fact that devices from many domains are entirely connected, the increasing usage of network infrastructure for creating secure connection between non-trivial tasks leads to complicated difficulties with security and trust. This domain does not require a trusted environment since sharing critical information is redundant. For example, the administrator does not allow devices to access any devices that are outside of the domain's range and do not have adequate authentication. However, there is a commonly used authentication approach for constructing a public-key infrastructure in which a third party is given certification that is used to provide root trust for all certifications. To reduce administrative costs, it is used for identity identification of multiple persons and other entities. Certificate authentication, on the other hand, is open to prospective attacks and prone to operational mistakes. With the evolution of blockchain, the consortium is assessed as a distributed ledger for maintaining a variety of communication mechanisms among nodes. Permission-based blockchains are those in which each network node must be vetted and authorised before being added to the network. The structure of the nodes' involvement is similar to that of a commercial partnership. The nodes are perfectly trustworthy; however, work collaboration and contracts are not regulated. It is used in a multiparty context as a variety of supporting methods. As a result, the consortium blockchain is used to establish trust across different domains where each domain has its own node capability for dealing with the global ledger. Figure 2.1 depicts a future webcast regarding the evolution. There are some drawbacks that are identified in various fields like storage limitations, privacy preservation, identity revocation, and so on [3].

The public infrastructure uses entity identification as a public key, which allows public revocation and inflexibility in the event of a private key breach. When a person claims to use email as a public key, it becomes more difficult to block continued usage of the email account if the private key is compromised. The identity of the node is occasionally revealed in order to provide a privacy-preserving entity. When malevolent nodes or adversaries may be easily expected, for example, it connects packets that are sent from one source and received from another source with a variety of services or people with whom it communicates. Similarly, as a newer level of transactions is authenticated and confirmed for providing the ledger, crypto methods may cause a variety of time lags. Because the size of the blocks is limited to a fixed size, storage restriction is considered a practical concern. These limitations are the result of a throughput bottleneck [4].

The major contribution is the prediction of an innovative and efficient safe crypto-based authentication technique (outbound supply chain authentication) that aids device authentication in IoT domains. With specific storage limits, the predicted model will need to cope with a storage mechanism that decreases the amount of data sent via the block chain and so reduces bottlenecks, overhead, and other issues. The experimental results show that the predicted outbound supply chain authentication model is efficient and effective.

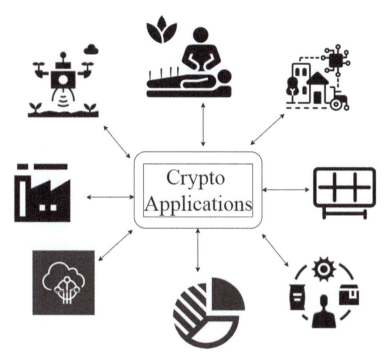

FIGURE 2.1 Crypto-based applications.

2.2 REVIEW OF LITERATURE

Some of the most common IoT environments are comprised of incompatible, highly separated, and highly linked devices. Centralised architectural processing is based on cloud computing, which is utilised to handle massive data flows across various data processing methods. A cyber-physical system (CPS)-centric biometric alternative, according to Shen et al. [5], will provide resourceful storage and unequalled processing efficiency. The author proposes to provide hadoop-based cloud computing services to improve data processing efficiency. The cloud computing (CC) environment outperforms a centralised environment in terms of storage and computing. It does not promote the use of security mechanisms or edge processing. Shen et al. [6] looked at the many functions of IoT from a different angle and proposed a number of important mechanisms for helping IoT, such as CC, radio-frequency identification (RFID), and social networking. Because of its network capabilities and device mobility, privacy protection and information security are two distinct concerns in IoT.

For IoT security authentication, a variety of unique protocols and networking techniques are utilised, such as mutual and lightweight authentication mechanisms, cluster-based constrained authentication key management, mutual message authentication protocol, and so on. IoT is also utilised to cope with scalability and flexibility difficulties. As a result, certain acceptable ways for dealing with these challenges, such as cryptocurrency, exist. The blockchain concept was born out of a need to provide trustworthy authentication and privacy protection services. Decentralised storage, distributed ledger, and distributed services based on a contract mechanism are three aspects that drive crypto adoption. Guizani et al., for example, created a variety of autonomous crypto environments to choose the most convincing electrical terminology. In order to provide conditional security for linked terminals, the author focused on a privacy-preserving network model. Chen et al. predicted crypto-based microgrid transactions. A network is used to make real-time monitoring and device certification easier.

In a cloud-based crypto system, authentication efficiency is a particularly difficult problem to address. Saravanan et al. [7] emphasise the importance of crypto security in a CC environment using a software-defined network. The present author focuses on leveraging smart contracts to solve the challenge of trust in a CC-based IoT ecosystem. The present author envisions interactions between miners and cloud providers as a game strategy for solving price problems and managing resources. A specialised device, on the other hand, must assure data veracity in order to reduce computing costs and resources (energy). Edge computing is used to promote edge processing since it is considered a newer computing paradigm. Edge computing, mobile terminals, and fixed infrastructures all have storage capacity and computational functionality that is dispersed [8-16].

The author looks at the advantages of using crypto to provide various mobile IoT systems. The author also describes a revolutionary mobile-based edge computing approach that uses a wireless crypto structural model to offload computationally heavy mining ideas to edge nodes. In addition, the author's approach ignores the authentication system. Moosai et al. predict a unique safe authentication strategy based on crypto and modelling for 5G dense situations [17]. Saravanan et al. [18] and colleagues developed a decentralised platform for providing data measurement and storage across a grounded IoT network topology. It also focuses on data security and cooperation sharing across various IoT contexts, which are not taken into account in the suggested paradigm. The present author proposes a block-chain-based Enterprise as a Service (EaaS) framework for energy trading in virtual to virtual (V2V) communication, which aims to improve the Software-Defined Networking (SDN) network paradigm. Cai et al. [19] describe a distributed environment blockchain-based authentication system. Cross-domain authentication, on the other hand, eliminates the resource constraints and inefficiency of cryptography.

While crypto-enabled IoT networks can satisfy the services and demands of next-generation networks, the gap analysis presented in this chapter identifies specific areas where more effort is needed. Based on these findings, the study recommends using reinforcement learning (RL) approaches to overcome some of the key challenges with crypto-enabled IoT networks. Two goals are to reduce block time and increase transaction throughput. Following this is a thorough case study in which a Q-learning method is utilised to decrease transmission delays for a miner, reducing the risk of forking situations. The statistics for the average transmission time pertaining to forking occurrences were compiled after extensive computations. The findings demonstrate that the Q-learning technique beats the greedy method while staying reasonably straightforward [20] [21–32].

According to Industry 4.0, digital cognitive computers outperform people when it comes to gathering and analysing data in real time, as well as sharing information that may help businesses make faster choices. The IoT includes intelligent assets that send and store data, data transmission infrastructures, and analytics. Because the IoT network has so many components, security breaches are more likely. Concerns about privacy and trustworthiness must be addressed. Crypto technology has lately experienced significant growth as a result of its trustworthy existence. We offer a crypto-based IoT architecture in this chapter with the goal of tackling a number of critical security challenges.

To summarise this study, there is a large body of work that focuses on blockchain systems in order to achieve various individual features such as system transparency, anonymity, and decentralisation. Furthermore, the IoT ecosystem pays relatively little attention to establishing authentication. As a result, the goal of this project is to develop an efficient authentication mechanism for IoT devices based on cryptography. Crypto provides effective authentication and resolution services in the IoT area. As a result, a novel proposal for improving the authentication process is presented.

2.3 THE PROPOSED METHODOLOGY

The proposed outbound supply chain authentication technique is discussed in this section. The crypto model builds confidence among the administrative domains that are offered and offers state binding to domain-specific information. It's a widely used authentication system. Device authentication is exploited through the key setup method. The verification step is used to ensure that the public key created by the signature is legitimate. Key generation, authentication, and crypto agents are grouped together in IoT to distinguish the layers depending on their functionality. The crypto layer serves as a secure conduit for transferring domain-specific information. With binding values and a domain identification made up of uniform identifiers and hash values, the crypto only keeps the bare minimum of information. The entity layer is made up of a number of components, including cryptographic systems like key generation and IoT. The key generation process is one of a kind, and it is in charge of keeping track of the private key for all IoT devices. Authentication and crypto agent servers make up the agent layer. To provide authentication functionality, the key generation procedure is carried out at the authentication layer. Verification and key creation are the two steps in the process. Domains in a crypto server must keep track of the enclosed mechanism's ledger. For the authentication procedure, information is gathered from different domains.

Blocks contain the number of transactions with domain-specific information to various administrative domains in the crypto layer. The ledger keeps track of the nodes that have been pre-selected to represent the administrative domains. With the right signature private key, the entities must be authenticated. Authentication can only be done with a single pass.

2.3.1 Signature Generation

A ring signature system uses the public keys of all users on a set U and a single private key of a user on U. Because of the ring signature's untraceability property, it may be utilised in anonymous payment applications or transactions. There is no reliable signature hub, the signer is completely anonymous, and there are significant exceptions. The security of this signature system is higher than that of the previous one. Even if attacker A has access to all of the members' private keys, he is unable to identify the signer. Attacker A cannot construct the message's ring signature from any non-zero probability since the likelihood of discovering the genuine signer is 1/n (n being the total number of ring members). In general, a successful ring signature can meet the following security requirements:

- Complete anonymity with no strings attached. Additionally, if an intruder illegally acquires the private keys of all prospective signers, he will compute that the true signer's likelihood is less than 1/n.
- Indestructible. Even if an external attacker acquires the signature of a message m from a random predictor that generates a ring signature, the chances of forging a legitimate signature remain slim.
- Without the help of a trusted third party or group administrator, the signer will design his own anonymous scope, construct a wonderful circular logical structure, and fulfil the main function of group signature.

Digital signatures can be used to verify the authenticity of a file or message. It is a form of non-repudiation in a way. Figures 2.1 and 2.2 shows a common digital signature method based on Ron Rivest, Adi Shamir and Leonard Adleman (RSA). It is one of the most widely used algorithms for digital signatures. The qualities of the crypto system may be well suited to digital signature systems. It will be safer and more relevant than traditional application areas, with the potential to grow in prominence. A digital signature, for example, just sends data across the internet and has no value.

2.3.2 Numerical Results and Discussions

Simulation is carried out in a MATLAB® environment, and metrics such as authentication time, distributed authentication time for peer channels, average latency, and hit ratio are calculated. The intensity of the number of edge nodes is supplied to crypto's edge nodes. Two additional authentication models are compared to the predicted outbound supply chain authentication paradigm in this chapter. There are two of them: a random cache and a popular cache. In the previous paradigm, the content is chosen at random by the edge nodes based on their capacity (Tables 2.1–2.4). Similarly, the caching procedure in the latter model is done with a belief propagation model to improve allocation efficiency. The analysis is carried out using a variety of factors based on popular and random caching, as well as average latency and hit ratio.

The authentication time is measured in milliseconds in Figure 2.3, which shows a graphical depiction of the authentication procedure. The x-axis shows the number of authenticated terminals. The figures are analysed in order to determine

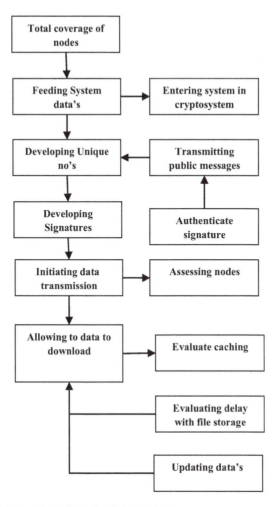

FIGURE 2.2   Crypto outbound supply chain mechanism.

TABLE 2.1
Authentication Time Computation Table

S.No	No. of Authentication Terminals	Authentication Time (ms)
1	5	200
2	10	400
3	15	600
4	20	800
5	25	1000
6	30	1200
7	35	1400
8	40	1600
9	45	1800

TABLE 2.2
Distributed Authentication Time Table

S.No	Terminal Number	Authentication Time (ms)
1	5	4
2	10	8
3	15	14
4	20	10
5	25	7
6	30	6
7	35	4
8	40	3
9	45	4

TABLE 2.3
Average Delay Computation Table

S.No	Maximum Amount of Terminals	Outbound Supply Chain	Popular Cache	Random Cache
1	100	2.8	3.9	4.5
2	150	2.9	3.8	4.6
3	200	2.6	3.7	4.7
4	250	2.7	3.5	4.5
5	300	2.9	3.9	4.3
6	350	2.9	3.7	4.4
7	400	2.7	3.5	4.7

TABLE 2.4
Average Hit Ratio Computation Table

S.No	Maximum Amount of terminals	Outbound Supply Chain	Popular Cache	Random Cache
1	100	1	0.5	0.01
2	150	0.96	0.53	0.03
3	200	0.75	0.55	0.05
4	250	0.8	0.57	0.07
5	300	0.65	0.58	0.09
6	350	0.5	0.61	0.11
7	400	0.42	0.65	0.17

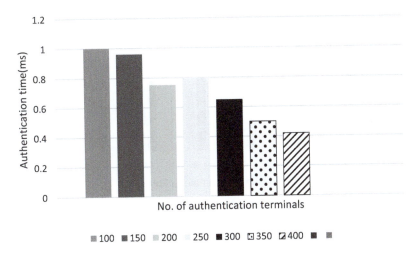

FIGURE 2.3 Authentication time computation.

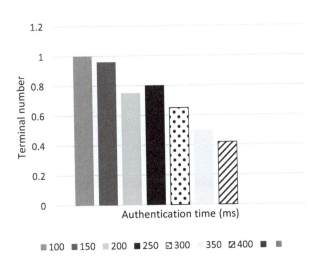

FIGURE 2.4 Distributed authentication time.

the authentication time. Six peers took 188 milliseconds, 385 milliseconds, 545 milliseconds, 780 milliseconds, 980 milliseconds, 1,175 milliseconds, 1,380 milliseconds, 1,565 milliseconds, and 1,755 milliseconds to authenticate. The authentication time for ten peers is 235 milliseconds, 480 milliseconds, 755 milliseconds, 995 milliseconds, 1,250 milliseconds, 1,495 milliseconds, 1,,755 milliseconds, 2,000 milliseconds, and 2,275 milliseconds, respectively. The terminal numbers are displayed on the y-axis, and the authentication time (ms) is plotted on the x-axis in Figure 2.4, which illustrates the distributed authentication time of six peers. 3 ms, 5 ms, 7 ms, 9 ms, 11 ms, 1 ms, 5 ms, 8 ms, and 9 ms, respectively, are the authentication

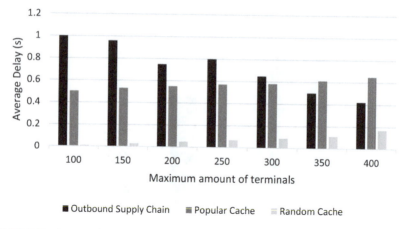

FIGURE 2.5 Average delay computation.

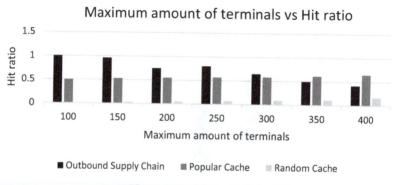

FIGURE 2.6 Average hit ratio computation.

times. The terminal numbers are displayed on the y-axis, and the authentication time (ms) is plotted on the x-axis in Figure 2.5, which displays the distributed authentication time of ten peers. The authentication times are 4 milliseconds, 8 milliseconds, 12 milliseconds, 10 milliseconds, 6 milliseconds, 4 milliseconds, and 2 milliseconds, respectively. The average delay computation is shown in Figure 2.6 with maximal terminals of 100, 150, 200, 250, 300, 350, and 400, respectively. The expected outbound supply chain authentication technique has a shorter average time than random and popular cache. The predicted model's average delay is 2.80 milliseconds, 2.85 milliseconds, 2.48 milliseconds, 2.58 milliseconds, 2.90 milliseconds, 2.86 milliseconds, and 2.50 milliseconds, respectively. The average hit ratio is depicted in Figure 2.6. Based on the study above, it is clear that the expected authentication model outperforms the other alternatives.

2.4 CONCLUSION

A unique blockchain-based security method called outbound supply chain authentication is expected developed in this study. It is used to provide a trust mechanism across different domains. The authentication procedure is used to ensure security. The outbound supply chain authentication solution ensures device privacy while allowing authentication across linked devices. Because of its flexible architecture, the system may be simply cancelled, and it authenticates entities to protect their privacy. To protect the data transmission route, a key generation process is used. The projected outbound supply chain model's performance is assessed in order to forecast system efficiency and security.

2.4.1 FUTURE SCOPE

Future research areas Crypto Operations Management for Industry 4.0 helps in numerous crypto-based data transmissions and in crypto currencies. The upcoming generations will be based on this secure data transmission. It uses the secure hashing and highly secure private key concepts for all the online events. It can be encapsulated with the hybrid artificial neural network models.

REFERENCES

[1] Shen, M., Tang, X., Zhu, L., Du, X., and Guizani, M., "Privacy-preserving support vector machine training over blockchain-based encrypted IoT data in smart cities," *IEEE Internet of Things Journal*, vol. 6, no. 5, pp. 7702–7712, Oct. 2019.

[2] Shen, M., Ma, B., Zhu, L., Mijumbi, R., Du, X., and Hu, J., "Cloud-based approximate constrained shortest distance queries over encrypted graphs with privacy protection," *IEEE Transactions on Information Forensics and Security*, vol. 13, no. 4, pp. 940–953, April 2018.

[3] Shen, M., Deng, Y., Zhu, L., Du, X., and Guizani, N., "Privacy-preserving image retrieval for medical iot systems: A blockchain-based approach," *IEEE Network*, vol. 33, no. 5, pp. 27–33, Sept. 2019.

[4] Saravanan, T., and Nithya, N.S., "Modeling displacement and direction aware ad hoc on-demand distance vector routing standard for mobile ad hoc networks," *Mobile Networks and Applications*, vol. 24, no. 6, pp. 1804–1813, 2019.

[5] Shen, M., Zhang, J., Zhu, L., Xu, K., and Tang, X., "Secure SVM training over vertically-partitioned datasets using consortium blockchain for vehicular social networks," *IEEE Transactions on Vehicular Technology*, vol. 69, no. 6, pp. 5773–5783, June 2019.

[6] Shen, M., Duan, J., Zhu, L., Zhang, J., Du, X., and Guizani, M., "Blockchain-based incentives for secure and collaborative data sharing in multiple clouds," *IEEE Journal on Selected Areas in Communications*, vol. 38, no. 6, pp. 1229–1241, June 2020.

[7] Saravanan, T., Saravanakumar, S., Rathinam, G., Narayanan, M., Poongothai, T., Patra, P. S. K., and Sengan, S. (2022). Malicious attack alleviation using improved time-based dimensional traffic pattern generation in UWSN. *Journal of Theoretical and Applied Information Technology*, 100(3).

[8] Saravanan, T., and Thillaiarasu, N., "Optimal grouping and belief based CH selection in mobile ad-hoc network using Chunk Reliable Routing Protocol," in *2021*

International Conference on Advance Computing and Innovative Technologies in Engineering (ICACITE) (pp. 933–940), March 2021. IEEE.

[9] Shi, W. et al., "Edge computing – an emerging computing model for the internet of everything era." *Journal of Computing Research and Development*, vol. 54, no. 5, pp. 907–924, 2017.

[10] Chaudhary R. et al., "BEST: Blockchain-based secure energy trading in SDN-enabled intelligent transportation system," *Computers and Security*, vol. 85, pp. 288–299, August 2019.

[11] Saravanan, T., and Nithya, N.S., "Mitigation of attack patterns based on routing reliance approach in MANETs," in *2020 2nd International Conference on Advances in Computing, Communication Control and Networking (ICACCCN)* (pp. 387–392). Dec. 2020. IEEE.

[12] Shen, W. et al., "Cooperative message authentication in vehicular cyber-physical systems," *IEEE Transactions on Emerging Topics in Computing*, vol. 1, no. 1, pp. 84–97, June 2018.

[13] Li, L. et al., "CreditCoin: A privacy-preserving blockchain-based incentive announcement network for communications of smart mobile terminals," *IEEE Transactions on Intelligent Transportation Systems*, vol. 19, no. 7, pp. 1–17, July 2018.

[14] Wang, W., Hu, N., and Liu, X., "BlockCAM: a blockchain-based cross-domain authentication model," *2018 IEEE Third International Conference on Data Science in Cyberspace (DSC)*, 2018, pp. 896–901.

[15] Li, J. et al., "Distributed caching for data dissemination in the downlink of heterogeneous networks," *IEEE Transactions on Communications*, vol. 63, no. 10, pp. 3553–3568, Oct. 2015.

[16] Thillaiarasu N., Gowthaman N., and Chenthur Pandian S., "Design of a confidentiality model using semantic-based information segmentation (SBIS) and scattered storage in cloud computing," in Nath Sur, S., Balas, V.E., Bhoi, A.K., and Nayyar, A. (eds.) *IoT and IoE Driven Smart Cities*. EAI/Springer Innovations in Communication and Computing. Springer, 2022. https://ur.b-ok.asia/book/18609045/6b2d19

[17] Moosavi, S. R., Gia, T. N., Rahmani, A.-M., Nigussie, E., Virtanen, S., Isoaho, J., and Tenhunen, H., "SEA: a secure and efficient authentication and authorization architecture for IoT-based healthcare using smart gateways," *Procedia Computer Science*, vol. 52, pp. 452–459, 2015.

[18] Saravanan, T., and Sasikumar, P. (2021), "Assessment and analysis of action degeneracy due to blackhole attacks in wireless sensor networks," in *Proceedings of 6th International Conference on Recent Trends in Computing: ICRTC 2020* (pp. 345–355). Springer Nature.

[19] Cai, H. et al., "IoT-based big data storage systems in cloud computing: perspectives and challenges," *IEEE Internet of Things Journal*, vol. 4, no. 1, pp. 75–87, Feb. 2017.

[20] Shi, W. et al., "Edge computing – an emerging computing model for the internet of everything era," *Journal of Computing Research and Development*, vol. 54, no. 5, pp. 907–924, 2017.

[21] Malini P., Gowthaman N., Gautami A., and Thillaiarasu N., "Internet of Everything (IoE) in smart city paradigm using advanced sensors for handheld devices and equipment," in Nath Sur, S., Balas, V.E., Bhoi, A.K., and Nayyar, A. (eds.) *IoT and IoE Driven Smart Cities*. EAI/Springer Innovations in Communication and Computing. Springer, 2022. https://ur.b-ok.asia/book/18609045/6b2d19

[22] Thillaiarasu N., Pandian S.C., and Gowthaman N., "Novel heuristic scheme to enforce safety and confidentiality using feature-based encryption in multi-cloud environment (MCE)," in Guarda, T., Anwar, S., Leon, M., and Mota Pinto, F.J. (eds) *Information*

and Knowledge in Internet of Things. EAI/Springer Innovations in Communication and Computing. Springer, 2022. https://ur.b-ok.asia/book/18609045/6b2d19

[23] Preethi, P. et al., "An effective digit recognition model using enhanced convolutional neural network based chaotic grey wolf optimization," *Journal of Intelligent & Fuzzy Systems*, vol. 41, no. 2, pp. 3727–3737, Sept. 2021.

[24] Thillaiarasu, N., Pandian, S.C., Vijayakumar, V. et al. Designing a trivial information relaying scheme for assuring safety in mobile cloud computing environment," *Wireless Networks*, vol. 27, 5477–5490, 2021. https://doi.org/10.1007/s11276-019-02113-4

[25] Thillaiarasu, N., and Chenthur Pandian, S., "A novel scheme for safeguarding confidentiality in public clouds for service users of cloud computing," *Cluster Computing*, vol. 22, 1179–1188, 2019. https://doi.org/10.1007/s10586-017-1178-8.

[26] Shyamambika, N., and Thillaiarasu, N., "A survey on acquiring integrity of shared data with effective user termination in the cloud," *2016 10th International Conference on Intelligent Systems and Control (ISCO)*, pp. 1–5, 2016. https://doi.org/10.1109/ISCO.2016.7726893.

[27] Thillaiarasu, N., and Chenthur Pandian, S., "Enforcing security and privacy over multicloud framework using assessment techniques," *2016 10th International Conference on Intelligent Systems and Control (ISCO)*, pp. 1–5, 2016. IEEE.

[28] Shyamambika, N., and Thillaiarasu. N., "Attaining integrity, secured data sharing and removal of misbehaving client in the public cloud using an external agent and secure encryption technique." *Advances in Natural and Applied Sciences*, vol. 10, no. 9 SE, pp. 421–432, 2016.

[29] Hao, Y., Chen, M., Hu, L. et al. "Energy efficient task caching and offloading for mobile edge computing," *IEEE Access*, vol. 6, pp. 11365–11373, 2018.

[30] Jameel, F., Javaid, U., Khan, W.U., Aman, M.N., Pervaiz, H., and Jäntti, R., "Reinforcement learning in blockchain-enabled IIoT networks: a survey of recent advances and open challenges," *Sustainability*, vol. 12, no. 12, 5161, 2020.

[31] Saravanan, T., and Nithya, N.S., "Modeling displacement and direction aware ad hoc on-demand distance vector routing standard for mobile ad hoc networks," *Mobile Networks and Applications*, vol. 24, no. 6, 1804–1813, 2019.

[32] Puri, V., Priyadarshini, I., Kumar, R., and Kim, L.C., "Blockchain meets IIoT: An architecture for privacy preservation and security in IIoT," in *2020 International Conference on Computer Science, Engineering and Applications (ICCSEA)*, pp. 1–7. March 2020. IEEE.

3 A Machine Learning-Based Approach for Fruit Grading and Classification

A. Diana Andrusia,[1] T. Mary Neebha,[1]
A. Trephena Patricia,[2] I. Thusnavis Bella Mary,[1]
and Hien Dang[3]
[1]Karunya Institute of Technology and Sciences,
Coimbatore, India
[2]Panimalar Engineering College, Chennai, India
[3]Faculty of Computer Science and Engineering, Thuy Loi
University, Hanoi, Vietnam

CONTENTS

3.1   INTRODUCTION

The application of computer vision and machine learning is growing rapidly in the field of agriculture. There are many automatic tasks involved with the pre- and post-harvesting stages of the agriculture field. Classification of diseases in the leaves is one of the tasks in the pre-harvesting stage. The grading of fruits and vegetables comes in the post-harvesting stages. Hence, in the area of agriculture there is a need to develop algorithms or methods to perform this task automatically.

DOI: 10.1201/9781003212201-4

Under machine vision, image processing plays a vital tool for analysing agriculture-based images. Automation techniques are very useful to farmers to predict the yield of an agriculture field and to know about a particular disease in crops. The machine vision-based methodology offers a non-destructive process for checking the external quality of agricultural products [1]. These methods usually calculate the quality parameters of the input with respect to the outer appearance of the product. Advancements in machine vision and communication can change the farmer's life in a beneficial way.

Computer vision-based applications in precise agriculture are growing steadily day by day. Food is the most important commodity in human life. Food producers are some of the most respected persons in the universe. Modern technologies and advanced systems are helpful for food producers to live better lives. The proposed research is such a kind of method to help food producers in a better way. In this chapter, the fruit grading and classification system is discussed in detail.

Fruit plays a vital role in human life because of its nutrition. It delivers natural substances to the human body. According to a UN Food and Agriculture Organization report, citrus is one of most popular, most produced and most consumed fruits in the world. Oranges come under the citrus family. According to the report, Brazil and the United States hold the first two positions in orange production. It is one of the major crops in India, ranking after bananas and mangos. The Indian states of Andhra Pradesh, Maharashtra, Rajasthan, Punjab, Karnataka and Haryana cultivate oranges more in comparison with other Indian states. The grading and classification processes of oranges are not automated in many countries.

Oranges have many beneficial aspects, one of which is they may be consumed in the form of fresh juice and jam. Vitamin C, minerals and natural sugars are available in it. Three hundred different varieties of oranges are available worldwide. All these varieties have peculiar properties such as shape, size, use and cost. The automatic grading of oranges may depend on the above properties of oranges. Modern industries and factories are leveraged with the usage of automatic classification systems. Hence, many researchers have researched the significant problems in fruit grading and classification. Following the Industrial Revolution, computer vision systems have been used recently to check the quality of the fruits. Fruits with stem ends cannot be properly classified by conventional machine vision methods. Variabilities in the inputs are not handled properly. So, modern industries have demanded advanced computer vision systems to handle the variety of inputs [2].

The growth of any plants is affected by many diseases and thereby may result in economic losses. So, it is better to identify diseases in earlier stages to avoid a severe impact on plants. The main diseases which affect orange fruits are brown rot, stubborn disease, citrus canker and melanoses. The identification of diseases and the grading of orange fruits are done by manual and computer vision–based methods. This chapter deals with the automatic classification and grading of oranges. The next section of the chapter discusses in detail the state-of-the-art methods related to fruit classification and grading.

3.2 BACKGROUND

Recently, many studies have been carried out in the field of fruit grading and classification. Notable findings have been gathered, to grade fruits based on the multiple and single features. The single features involve size, colour, shape and so forth. The accuracy level of single features methods is very low compared to multiple features methods [3]. A computer vision–based system was presented by Zhang et al. [4] to classify the types of 18 fruits. Input features such as shape, texture and colour are extracted from individual input images. The types of fruits were detected by a neural network–based classifier and 89.1% classification accuracy was obtained. The improvement methodology of Zhang et al. [4] was investigated by incorporating principal component analysis (PCA) as a feature reduction technique [5].

A radial basis function-based neural network was used to find the initial features of the input and thereby fruit classification was carried out [6]. An automatic apple grading system was developed by Bhatt el al. [7]. Artificial Neural Network (ANN)-based classification was performed. Initially, multi features of colour and size were obtained. Sethy et al. [8] investigated the disease classification of rice leaf. K-means clustering and SVM techniques were used to find the defective parts of rice leaf. The mineral deficiencies from leaf images were obtained with classification accuracies from 85% to 90%. The automatic grading of rice leaves was implemented based on fuzzy logic techniques [9]. Online grading of apples is performed through fusion techniques with respect to the image features [10].

Andrushia et al. [11] experimented with artificial bee colony (ABC)-based grape disease classification. The colour, shape and texture of 110 features were extracted in the initial phase. Afterwards, the optimal features were selected through ABC-based optimization. The optimal feature set was given to an SVM-based classifier for disease classification. Classification accuracy of 93.01% was obtained by utilizing the ABC method. For KNN-based classification, only 89.13% accuracy was obtained. The results were also compared with state-of-the-art optimization methods such as particle swarm optimization (PSO) and genetic algorithm (GA). The extraction of an optimal feature set from the original features played an important role. Chen et al. [12] utilized PSO and SVM for a fruit grading system. A discriminant tree-based analysis was used to find fruit diameter and defective portions of fruit. The grades of the fruits were categorized by fused decision making rules.

The different parts of oranges were analysed thoroughly in which the colour features of ripe and non-ripe oranges were extracted [12]. An automatic model was established to separate backgrounds and to grade the different oranges with respect to the data available in each colour model. The hyper spectral image-based system was investigated by Gómez-Sanchís et al. [13]. In the hyperspectral images, disease classification and segmentation of citrus fruit were performed. Initially, the input image acquisition was fully tuned by liquid crystal tunable filters.

Sabzi et al. [14] presented a computer vision–based method for orange grading tasks. Three classes of oranges, namely paybandi, bam and Thomson, were classified. In total, 300 images were used for the experiment. The important image features were selected by using three optimizations techniques. The orange varieties were graded with 96.7% classification accuracy. Sa'ad et al. [15] recorded a grading system for mango fruits. The pre-processing steps of enhancement, feature extraction and restoration were performed at the earlier stage. In addition, shape features were extracted directly from the inputs and provided to the classifier. Discriminant analysis and SVM were used to grade the mangoes. SVM-based classification has maximum accuracy compared to other methods.

The disease detection and classification of pomegranate fruits were discussed in Bhange et al. [16]. Under the smart farm scheme, the method was launched. Colour and morphological features were extracted initially. Defective and non-defective pomegranates were graded with an accuracy of 82%. This method was directly implemented in the fields in order to help farmers. Andrushia et al. [17] investigated mango skin disease classification. The important and optimal features were selected through ABC-based optimization. Two types of mango skin disease were identified by using the SVM classifier. Dutta et al. [18] investigated a method for classifying farm-fresh grapes and pesticide-affected grapes. The Haar transform was used to analyse the input images. The feature difference between the two types of grapes was calculated at the initial phase. SVM was adhered to, to classify the types of grape. The major phases of state-of-the-art grading and classification involve input acquisition, pre-processing, feature extraction, classification and post-processing. The proposed method also discusses major phases along with MSVM. Recently, convolution neural network (CNN)-based deep learning methods have been leveraged for fruit grading and classification. Deep learning methods require a large number of inputs to evaluate the performance of the techniques.

3.3 METHODOLOGY

The proposed framework for an orange fruit grading system consists of four phases. Pre-processing, feature extraction, classification and performance evaluation are the four major phases of the proposed method. A detailed flow chart is given in Figure 3.1.

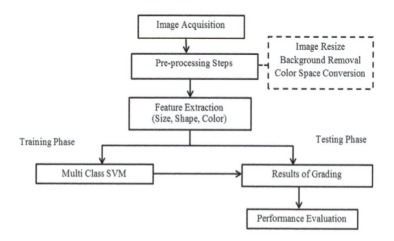

FIGURE 3.1 Flow chart for the proposed grading system.

3.3.1 IMAGE ACQUISITION

The orange images are collected from an online database [www.cofilab.com/portfo
lio/orangesdb/] [19–20] and from real-time orange images. The proposed method is
to experiment with 200 orange images. Under each grading category, 50 images are
taken for the proposed method. Eighty percent input is taken for the training phase
and 20% input is considered for the testing phase.

3.3.2 PRE-PROCESSING

Pre-processing is a mandatory step for most image-processing techniques. These
steps help the classifier identify the inputs under the correct class. The pre-processing
step of the proposed method consists of three steps, such as resizing, background
removal and colour space conversion. The input image is resized to the size of 256 x
256. After resizing, the input images are sharpened by a Laplacian operator.

3.3.2.1 Background Removal

The input image is represented in red, green, blue (RGB) colour space. The selection of colour space directly impacts the results of the background removal process.
RGB, HSI, LAB and YCbCr are the common colour models in the computer vision
applications. The Hue, Saturation, Intensity (HSI) colour model closely relates to
visualization by the human eye and nullifies the noisiness of illumination on colour.
So, the input image in the RGB colour space is converted into the HSI colour model.
 The conversion equations from RGB to HSI are given below:

$$H = arccos\left(\frac{0.5\left[(R-G)+(R-B)\right]}{\sqrt{\left[(R-G)^2 +(R-B)(G-B)\right]}} \right). \qquad (3.1)$$

$$S = 1 - \left(\frac{3}{(R+G+B)} \right)\left[\min(R,G,B)\right]. \qquad (3.2)$$

$$I = \frac{1}{3}(R+G+B). \qquad (3.3)$$

The intensity values of (R,G,B) lie between 0 to 255.

$$B > G\, then\, H = 360 - H. \qquad (3.4)$$

$$B \le G\, then\, H \in \{1,180\}. \qquad (3.5)$$

The histograms of H, S and I colour components are analysed to effectively eliminate
the backgrounds from the input fruit image. The individual components alone cannot

help in the background removal process. All the components together achieve the removal of backgrounds effectively. The background-free colour image is obtained by adding the binary image with the original input. The input orange images and background elimination images are shown in Figure 3.2.

3.3.2.2 Feature Extraction

The feature extraction phase represents the input images in efficient manner. Shape, colour and size features are extracted from input orange images. Shape is one of the vital appearance features of orange fruit. In order to define the shape feature, the level of circularity (L) is found in the proposed method. Both the sides of an orange are calculated with circularity, and the minimum value is taken as the final value. It is calculated by the following equation:

$$L = \frac{4\pi A}{s^2},$$

(3.6)

where A is the total number of pixels in the orange region (i.e. area of the orange), and S is the number of edge points in the orange.

A healthy orange fruit mostly in orange colour which uniformly appears throughout the surface of the fruit. Hence, the orange colour area to the total area of the fruit is considered for colour feature. In the HSI colour model, consists of colour information. In order to separate the orange area, a proper colour threshold is used. The final colour feature is calculated by the mean value of the orange area ratio on both sides of one fruit [1].

Size is another key feature for grading of fruit. The size of orange fruit is determined by considering two sides of the fruit. The maximum cross section is considered as mean diameter (m_d). Sobel and Canny edge detectors are used to find the edge pixels of the fruit (A_j, B_j). The fruit centroid coordinates are denoted by (O_x, O_y):

$$m_d = \frac{2}{T} \sum_{j=1}^{T} \left(\left(A_j - O_x \right)^2 + \left(B_j - O_y \right)^2 \right)^{\frac{1}{2}},$$

(3.7)

$$O_x = \frac{1}{T} \sum_{j=1}^{T} A_j,$$

(3.8)

$$O_y = \frac{1}{T} \sum_{j=1}^{T} B_j,$$

(3.9)

where T represents the sum of pixels at the end points of the orange fruit. The features of fruit colour, shape and size are normalized with a maximum and minimum value:

$$C_i = \frac{c - \min(c)}{\max(c) - \min(c)},$$

(3.10)

where c is feature attributes which vary from 1 to 4.

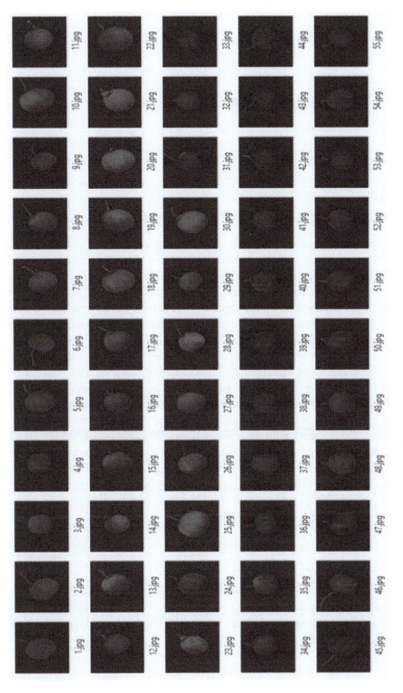

FIGURE 3.2 Sample images for proposed grading system.

The entropy-based texture features are calculated. This shows the uniformity and roughness of the input image. The entropy (E_i) is calculated by

$$E_i = -k \sum_{j=1}^{n} b_{ij} \ln b_{ij},$$ (3.11)

where $= \dfrac{1}{\ln n}$. Weighted entropy of the ith feature is calculated by

$$w_i = \frac{1 - E_i}{\sum_{i=1}^{n} \left(1 - E_i\right)}.$$ (3.12)

3.4 MULTI-CLASS SUPPORT VECTOR MACHINE (MSVM)

The important motivation of pattern classification is to select the model which enlarges the performance of the input data. Traditional learning methods correctly learn the input and classify what belongs to a particular class. The generalization ability is less. SVM is used essentially in both data mining and machine learning methods, and is mostly used by the researchers. A large variety of applied research, such as in finance, neuroscience, computer vision and text categorization, uses SVM. The success of SVM depends on the solving classification tasks.

SVM is one of the supervised learning strategies. The main goal of SVM is to classify several classes of training data. It maximizes the generalization ability of the model. It is based on the decision of hyper-planes and it paradigms liner functions from a training data set. The linear separator is constituted with maximum distance from the hyper-plane, which separates negative and positive samples. It results in mostly correct identification for the training data set and not for the testing data set.

SVM undergoes the objective of the structural risk minimization principle. In order to train SVM, a set of training samples is required. Let a_i be the input vector with associated label b_i. The training input set is given by

$$A = \left(a_1, b_1\right), \left(a_2, b_2\right), \left(a_3, b_3\right) \ldots\ldots \left(a_m, b_m\right),$$ (3.13)

(i.e. $A = \left\{a_i, b_i\right\}_{i=1}^{m}$). The two-dimensional image inputs are considered. The training data can be linearly separable and other types of hyper-planes are available to perform the separation. In general, the generalization ability depends on the maximum margin of the hyper-plane and its location [21–22]. The following equation is used to separate the inputs with the help of a hyper-plane:

$$W^T a_i + b = 0.$$ (3.14)

The kernel functions which are used in the SVM are linear, polynomial, Gaussian, radial basis function (RBF), and sigmoid. The performance of SVM differ with respect to kernel type. The selection of kernel depends on the characteristics of the input images, as more than one class exists in the output. So, in the proposed method, multi-class SVM is used for the classification phase. The feature vectors of training data are given to the MSVM. The grading of oranges depends on a multi-class problem. Hence, MSVM is leveraged in the proposed method. The real-time grading system does not have only two classes, such as healthy and defective. A detailed grading system will help in the fruit packing industry. In order to classify fruits accurately, four categories are followed in the proposed method. The grading categories are Good (grade A), Moderate (grade B), Bad (grade C), and very Bad (grade D). The MSVM technique one-against-all is used in the proposed method [23–24].

Posterior probability is used to distinguish each response under the one-against-all method [25]. The modified sigmoid activation function is given to the SVM classifier.

Let $f_i(x)$ be the output of SVM after the training stage, and φ_i be the training classes:

$$P(\varphi_i \mid f_{i(x)}) = \frac{1}{1 + e^{\left(\alpha_i \mid f_{i(x)} + \beta_i\right)}}.$$

(3.15)

α_i and β_i are calculated by reducing the local likelihood Equation (3.16)

$$-\sum_{m=1}^{n} t_m \log\left(p_m\right) + \left(1 + t_m\right) \log\left(1 - p_m\right),$$

(3.16)

where p_m and t_m are the output of the sigmoid function and the target of probability. The posterior probability of the one-against-all method is also encountered by another activation function. The generalization of the sigmoid function is the softmax function which is used in MSVM:

$$P(\varphi_i \mid x) = \frac{e^{\left(\alpha_i \mid f_{i(x)} + \beta_i\right)}}{\sum_{i=1}^{c} e^{\left(\alpha_i \mid f_{i(x)} + \beta_i\right)}}.$$

(3.17)

The sigmoid and softmax functions are used as activation functions for MSVM training. Four categories of inputs are used for training. The training parameters are set to form an unbiased data set. Detailed steps of the MSVM implementation are given below:

- Constitute M binary SVM.
- Each one separates a particular class from other classes.
- Using jth class samples, train the jth SVM as positive labels. Negative labels are five for other training samples.

3.5   RESULTS AND DISCUSSION

The proposed method is implemented on a personal computer with a 2.90 GHZ Processor, 12GB RAM and MATLAB®. The proposed method uses 200 orange images which were collected from an online database and real-time orange images. Four-category grading is implemented. Figure 3.2 shows the sample orange images for the proposed grading method.

The background removal and colour space conversion are the major components of the pre-processing phase. The entire image is resized to 256 × 256. Figure 3.3 shows the binary images of input after the pre-processing steps. The histogram analysis of the H component, S component and I component is given in Figure 3.4. The results of histogram are shown in Figure 3.5. The bimodal curve of HSI components exist in the histogram plot of the inputs. The HSI components are used to eliminate the backgrounds. The HSI components together lead the effective background removal process.

3.5.1   PERFORMANCE ANALYSIS

The proposed grading system is analysed in terms performance metrics. The grading accuracy of the proposed method is evaluated for four grading classes such as Good

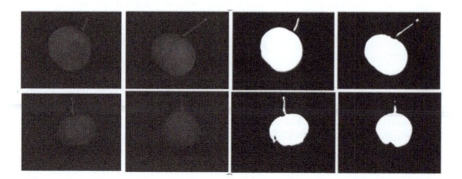

FIGURE 3.3   Results of pre-processing stage.

FIGURE 3.4   Images in HIS colour space.

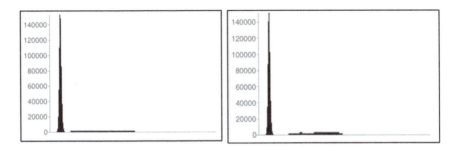

FIGURE 3.5   Histogram of colour components.

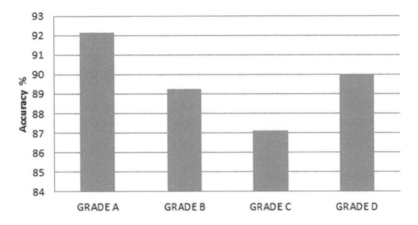

FIGURE 3.6   Grading accuracy of KNN.

(Grade A), Moderate (Grade B), Bad (Grade C), and very Bad (Grade D). It mostly depends on the total number of images which are correctly classified. The grading accuracy is calculated by the following equation:

$$GA = \frac{Number\,of\,correctly\,graded\,images}{Total\,images\,in\,testing\,phase} \times 100. \qquad (3.18)$$

The proposed method for a grading system is implemented by MSVM. In addition, the K-Nearest Neighbour classifier is also used to make the evaluation. It classifies unknown instances, which are ultimately based on the similarity function [26–27]. The training and testing images for MSVM and KNN are same. The grading accuracy of the proposed method through MSVM and KNN is highlighted in Figures 3.6 and 3.7.

Figures 3.6 and 3.7 highlight the grading accuracy for the four classes. For the first category of 'GRADE A', KNN and MSVM classifiers provide good grading accuracy. However, for the other grades, KNN fails to classify to the particular class. This is due

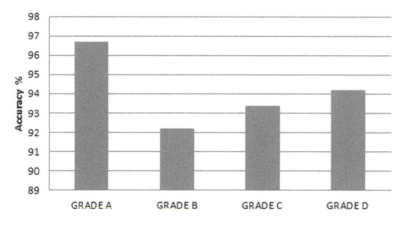

FIGURE 3.7   Grading accuracy of MSVM.

to the large amount of data and sensitivity to the input image scale. Normalization of input is needed for KNN and hence, it produces lesser accuracy for different GRADES. Thus, MSVM classifies extremely well for 'GRADE C' and 'GRADE D'. The proposed fruit grading system provides better results for all four categories by using MSVM.

3.5.2   COMPARATIVE ANALYSIS

The proposed method of a grading system is compared with other state-of-the-art methods. The comparison methods are carefully chosen in order to perform a fair comparison Elhariri et al. (2014) proposed a method for a tomato grading system using MSVM. A classification accuracy of 92.72% was achieved with the Elhariri et al. [28] method. The linear kernel function was used to perform the classification. The proposed method used the modified kernel function in the classifier. Henceforth, the accuracy of the proposed method is enhanced in comparison with the Elhariri et al. [28] method.

A weighted K-means clustering-based apple grading system was proposed by Yu et al. [1]. Recognition accuracy of 96% was obtained with this method. Zhang and Zhang (2016) proposed a binary particle swarm optimization-based apple grading system. However, the processing time of the method is low. Yong et al. [29] investigated an apple grading system by incorporating PSO. These state-ot-the-art comparison methods show that the proposed method achieves good grading accuracy of 96.7%. Table 3.1 summarizes the performance metrics comparison with state-of-the-art methods [31–34].

3.6   CONCLUSIONS

This chapter deals with a grading system for oranges by using the MSVM machine learning technique. The machine vision-based system is highly useful in the post-harvesting stage. The chapter contributes four categories of grading systems for

TABLE 3.1
Comparison of Classification Accuracy with State-of-the-Art Methods

Methods	Model	Classification Accuracy (%)
Esraa Elhariri et al. [28]	MSVM	92.72
Y. Yu et al. [1]	Weighted K-means Clustering	96
Jian Zhang et al. [30]	BPSO	98
Y. Yong et al. [29]	PSO	95
Proposed	MSVM	96.7

orange fruit. Pre-processing, feature extraction and classification are the three major blocks of the proposed method. The major features of circularity, shape, size and colour are considered for feature extraction. MSVM is used for classification under four categories. The quantitative and qualitative results are highlighted in the proposed method. The performance of the proposed method is compared with four state-of-the-art fruit grading methods. The proposed method yields a grading accuracy of 96.7%. This research can be extended by incorporating industrial IoT concepts for automatic fruit packaging applications.

REFERENCES

1. Razmjooy, N., Mousavi, B. S., & Soleymani, F. (2012). A real-time mathematical computer method for potato inspection using machine vision. *Computers & Mathematics with Applications, 63*(1), 268–279.
2. Li, J., Rao, X., Wang, F., Wu, W., & Ying, Y. (2013). Automatic detection of common surface defects on oranges using combined lighting transform and image ratio methods. *Postharvest Biology and Technology, 82*, 59–69.
3. Yu, Y., Velastin, S. A., & Yin, F. (2020). Automatic grading of apples based on multi-features and weighted K-means clustering algorithm. *Information Processing in Agriculture, 7*(4), 556–565.
4. Zhang, Y., Wang, S., Ji, G., & Phillips, P. (2014). Fruit classification using computer vision and feedforward neural network. *Journal of Food Engineering, 143*, 167–177.
5. Zhang, Y., Phillips, P., Wang, S., Ji, G., Yang, J., & Wu, J. (2016). Fruit classification by biogeography-based optimization and feedforward neural network. *Expert Systems, 33*(3), 239–253.
6. Liang, M., & Meng, D. W. (2012). Application of multi-feature image fusion apple grading method. *Computer Simulation, 29*, 256–259.
7. Bhatt, A. K., & Pant, D. (2015). Automatic apple grading model development based on back propagation neural network and machine vision, and its performance evaluation. *AI & Society, 30*(1), 45–56.
8. Sethy, P. K., Kumari, C., Barpanda, N., Negi, B., Behera, S., & Kuma Rath, A. (2017). Identification of mineral deficiency in rice crop based on SVM in approach of k-means & fuzzy c-means clustering. *Helix, 7*(5), 1970–1983.
9. Sethy, P. K., Negi, B., Barpanda, N. K., Behera, S. K., & Rath, A. K. (2018). Measurement of disease severity of rice crop using machine learning and computational intelligence. In Sasikumar Gurumoorthy, Bangole Narendra Kumar Rao, &

Xiao-Zhi Gao (Eds.), *Cognitive science and artificial intelligence* (pp. 1–11). Springer Singapore.

10. Huang, C., & Fei, J. (2017). Online apple grading based on decision fusion of image features. *Transactions of the Chinese Society of Agricultural Engineering, 33*(1), 285–291.

11. Andrushia, A. D., & Patricia, A. T. (2020). Artificial bee colony optimization (ABC) for grape leaves disease detection. *Evolving Systems, 11*(1), 105–117.

12. Chen, Y., Wu, J., & Cui, M. (2018, December). Automatic classification and detection of oranges based on computer vision. In *2018 IEEE 4th International Conference on Computer and Communications (ICCC)* (pp. 1551–1556). IEEE.

13. Gómez-Sanchís, J., Lorente, D., Soria-Olivas, E., Aleixos, N., Cubero, S., & Blasco, J. (2014). Development of a hyperspectral computer vision system based on two liquid crystal tuneable filters for fruit inspection. Application to detect citrus fruits decay. *Food and Bioprocess Technology, 7*(4), 1047–1056.

14. Shyamambika, N., & Thillaiarasu, N. (2016). A survey on acquiring integrity of shared data with effective user termination in the cloud. In *2016 10th International Conference on Intelligent Systems and Control (ISCO)* (pp. 1–5). IEEE Explore. https://doi.org/10.1109/ISCO.2016.7726893.

15. Sabzi, S., Abbaspour-Gilandeh, Y., & García-Mateos, G. (2018). A new approach for visual identification of orange varieties using neural networks and metaheuristic algorithms. *Information Processing in Agriculture, 5*(1), 162–172.

16. Sa'ad, F. S. A., Ibrahim, M. F., Shakaff, A. M., Zakaria, A., & Abdullah, M. Z. (2015). Shape and weight grading of mangoes using visible imaging. *Computers and Electronics in Agriculture, 115*, 51–56.

17. Bhange, M., & Hingoliwala, H. A. (2015). Smart farming: Pomegranate disease detection using image processing. *Procedia Computer Science, 58*, 280–288.

18. Andrushia, A. D., & Patricia, A. T. (2019). Artificial bee colony based feature selection for automatic skin disease identification of mango fruit. In Jude Hemanth & Valentina Emilia Balas (Eds.), *Nature inspired optimization techniques for image processing applications* (pp. 215–233). Springer, Cham.

19. Dutta, M. K., Sengar, N., Minhas, N., Sarkar, B., Goon, A., & Banerjee, K. (2016). Image processing based classification of grapes after pesticide exposure. *LWT-Food Science and Technology, 72*, 368–376.

20. Vidal, A., Talens, P., Prats-Montalbán, J. M., Cubero, S., Albert, F., & Blasco, J. (2013). In-line estimation of the standard colour index of citrus fruits using a computer vision system developed for a mobile platform. *Food and Bioprocess Technology, 6*(12), 3412–3419.

21. Cubero, S., Diago, M. P., Blasco, J., Tardáguila, J., Millán, B., & Aleixos, N. (2014). A new method for pedicel/peduncle detection and size assessment of grapevine berries and other fruits by image analysis. *Biosystems Engineering, 117*, 62–72.

22. Liu, Y., & Zheng, Y. F. (2005). One-against-all multi-class SVM classification using reliability measures. In *Proceedings. 2005 IEEE International Joint Conference on Neural Networks* (Vol. 2, 849–854). IEEE.

23. Thillaiarasu N., Pandian S. C., & Gowthaman N. (2022) Novel heuristic scheme to enforce safety and confidentiality using feature-based encryption in multi-cloud environment (MCE). In T. Guarda, S. Anwar, M. Leon, & F. J. Mota Pinto (Eds.), *Information and knowledge in Internet of Things* EAI/Springer Innovations in Communication and Computing (pp. 441–456). Springer, Cham. https://doi.org/10.1007/978-3-030-75123-4_20

24. Cervantes, J., Garcia-Lamont, F., Rodríguez-Mazahua, L., & Lopez, A. (2020). A comprehensive survey on support vector machine classification: Applications, challenges and trends. *Neurocomputing, 408*, 189–215.
25. Aiolli, F., Sperduti, A., & Singer, Y. (2005). Multiclass classification with multi-prototype support vector machines. *Journal of Machine Learning Research, 6*(5), 817–850.
26. Zhang, S., Wang, H., & Huang, W. (2017). Two-stage plant species recognition by local mean clustering and weighted sparse representation classification. *Cluster Computing, 20*(2), 1517–1525.
27. Preethi, P. et al. (2021). An effective digit recognition model using enhanced convolutional neural network based chaotic grey wolf optimization. *Journal of Intelligent & Fuzzy Systems, 41*(2), 3727–3737.
28. Thillaiarasu, N., Chenthur Pandian, S. (2019). A novel scheme for safeguarding confidentiality in public clouds for service users of cloud computing. *Cluster Computing, 22*, 1179–1188. https://doi.org/10.1007/s10586-017-1178-8
29. Devi, T. G., & Neelamegam, P. (2019). Image processing based rice plant leaves diseases in Thanjavur, Tamilnadu. *Cluster Computing, 22*(6), 13415–13428.
30. Keerthana, P., Geetha, B. G., & Kanmani, P. (2017). Crustose using shape features and color histogram with K nearest neighbor classifiers. *International Journal of Innovations in Scientific and Engineering Research (IJISER), 4*(9), 199–203.
31. Dubey, A. K., Gupta, U., & Jain, S. (2016). Analysis of k-means clustering approach on the breast cancer Wisconsin dataset. *International Journal of Computer Assisted Radiology and Surgery, 11*(11), 2033–2047.
32. Elhariri, E., El-Bendary, N., Fouad, M. M. M., Platoš, J., Hassanien, A. E., & Hussein, A. M. (2014). Multi-class SVM based classification approach for tomato ripeness. In Václav Snášel, Ajith Abraham, Pavel Krömer, Millie Pant, & Azah Kamilah Muda (Eds.), *Innovations in bio-inspired computing and applications* (pp. 175–186). Springer, Cham.
33. Yin, Y., Tao, K., & Yu, H. (2012). Feature selection method for apple grading based on machine vision. *Nongye Jixie Xuebao = Transactions of the Chinese Society for Agricultural Machinery, 43*(6), 118–121.
34. Zhang, J., & Zhang, L. (2016). Multi-feature extraction of apple grading based on improved binary particle swarm optimization algorithm. *Acta Agriculturae Zhejiangensis, 28*(9), 1609–1615.

4 Artificial Intelligence Impact on Pattern Classification in Association with IoT for Advanced Applications

E.B. Priyanka,[1] S. Thangavel,[1] G. Manikandan,[2] and C.V. Rahav[1]*
[1]Department of Mechatronics Engineering,
Kongu Engineering College, Perundurai, India
[2]Department of Automobile Engineering,
Kongu Engineering College, Perundurai, India

CONTENTS

4.1   INTRODUCTION

Pattern acknowledgment can be considered as a cycle of characterization in which the point is to remove designs from an information set and order them into various classes. Pattern recognition (PR) is concerned with the plan and advancement of frameworks that perceive designs in information. Along these lines, the motivation behind a PR framework is to dissect and portray a scene in reality which is helpful for the achievement of a specific assignment. The genuine perceptions arranged by a PR framework are gathered through sensors. Throughout the long term, a few meanings of PR have been given. Watanabe [1] characterizes an example "as inverse of a tumult; it is an element, dubiously characterized, that could be given a name". Further, in order to resolve a complex situation, PR will serve as a better field to identify the normal or abnormal behavior of the system in an efficient manner. Concerned with machine acknowledgment of important normalities in boisterous or complex conditions, for PR is an overall term to portray a wide scope of issues, for example, acknowledgment, depiction, characterization, and gathering of examples. In his book, Pavlidis (1977) insisted that "the word design is gotten from a similar root as the word supporter and, in his unique use, it suggests something which is set up as an ideal guide to be imitated. Hence, PR suggests the ID of the ideal which a given article was made after". In late examination, PR is a grouping of information through the extraction of significant highlights from a parcel of uproarious dataware [2]. As indicated by Fukunaga, PR can be characterized as "an issue of assessing thickness capacities in a high-dimensional space and isolating the space into the districts of classes of classes" [8]. Schalkoff characterized PR as "the science that worries the depiction or arrangement (acknowledgment) of estimations". Consequently, it is obvious from these definitions that PR alludes to the forecast of the obscure idea of a perception, a discrete amount, for example, dark or white, one or zero, wiped out or sound, genuine or then again phony [3].

Specifically, the accompanying perspectives are formulated for PR: meaning of example classes, detecting condition, design portrayal, highlight extraction and determination, group examination, classifier plan and learning, choice of preparing and test tests, and execution assessment. The difficult data veracity directs the selection of sensors, pre-handling strategies, portrayal plan, and dynamic model [4]. The utilization of PR is concerned with a few fields of examination and instances of this can be found in an assortment of building and logical controls, for example, in science, medicine, promotion, PC vision, and furthermore, computerized reasoning. In various up-and-coming applications, it is clear that no single methodology for characterization is "ideal," and furthermore, that various techniques and approaches have been utilized [5]. Thus, the combination of a few detecting procedures and classifiers is presently a regularly utilized practice in PR. It is by and large concurred that a fully established framework and acknowledged sequence flow will be identified with minimum downtime presentation. A very much characterized and adequately compelled acknowledgment issue (few intraclass varieties and enormous interclass varieties) is probably going to prompt a reduced example presentations and, furthermore, a straightforward dynamic methodology [6]. Because of the expanding consideration paid to PR-based applications, there are as of now a couple of extensive diagrams and deliberate mappings of PR applications plans. The invisibility of the dataware house schematics layout looks at the highlights of PR and how they have been created. Rather, existing surveys investigate in detail an explicit space, procedure, or framework, zeroing in on the calculations and also procedure subtleties. In order to close the previously mentioned gap, this chapter presents a deliberate survey to investigate the multidisciplinary nature of calculations and strategies of PR-based applications [7].

4.2   TECHNIQUES FOR PATTERN RECOGNITION USING MACHINE LEARNING—OVERVIEW

AI advanced from the collaborative analysis of PR and computational learning hypothesis and is especially concerned with the execution of utilizations that can learn and furthermore make expectations with respect to new information in a self-sufficient way. Specifically, in directed learning, an objective capacity is identified and it is used to anticipate the estimations of a discrete class quality as endorsed or then again discarded, for instance, when there are name instances of at least two classes (for example, malady versus sound). AI calculations make forecasts for a given arrangement of tests, though directed learning calculations look for designs inside the esteem marks relegated to information focuses [8]. These calculations are comprised of a result variable which must be predicted from the initial image, that is, a given arrangement of indicators or free factors. By utilizing this variable set, it is conceivable to produce a capacity that maps contributions to wanted yields. The preparation cycle proceeds until the model accomplishes a degree of precision on the preparation information. Models of administered learning calculations are: uphold vector machine (SVM), irregular woods (RF), choice tree, neural organizations, knearest neighbors (kNN), naïve Bayes (NB), and virtual neural organization (ANN) [9]. As summed up in Figure 4.1, the present study targets characterizing research distributed in the fields of AI, measurable technique, and profound picking up as indicated by a few viewpoints so as to analyze the application evaluation of these techniques and recognize their focal points and burdens. In the accompanying subsections, every technique introduced in Figure 4.1 is examined [10].

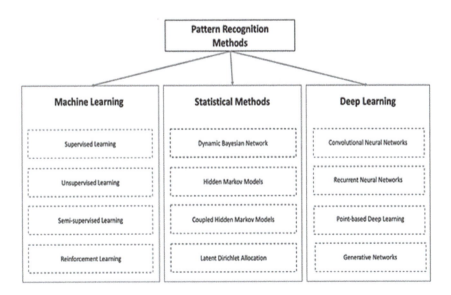

FIGURE 4.1   PR methods with respect to ML, DL and SM algorithms.

The administered learning is partitioned into two stages: training (learning a model utilizing the preparation information) and testing the model (utilizing concealed test information to determine model exactness). The calculations gain from past understanding and endeavor to catch the most ideal information to settle on precise choices [11]. Solo getting the hang of (bunching) is a troublesome issue for various reasons, for example, successful likeness measures, model capacities, calculations, and introductory conditions. Solo calculations are utilized when the examples are not marked. These calculations depend on a learning approach where examples are consequently positioned into significant gatherings dependent on their similitude, and the classifier is planned by deriving existing examples or bunches in the preparation informational indexes. For the most part, calculations of bunching can be ordered into dividing techniques, various leveled strategies, thickness-based techniques, lattice-based techniques, and model-based techniques [12]. The parceling strategies are isolated into two significant subcategories, the centroid and the medoid calculations. The centroid calculations speak to each bunch by utilizing the gravity focus of the occurrences. The medoid calculations speak to each group by methods for the examples nearest to the gravity focus.

Conventional bunching approaches produce allotments, and in a parcel each example has a place with one and only one group. Fluffy grouping expands this idea; partner each example with each group utilizing an enrollment work. Bigger enrollment esteems show higher trust in the task of the example to the bunch. One generally utilized calculation is the fluffy C-implies (FCM) calculation, which depends on k-implies [13]. FCM distinguishes the most trademark point in each bunch, which can be considered as the "middle" of the group and, at that point, distinguishes the evaluation of enrollment for each occurrence in the bunches. Other delicate grouping calculations have been created and a large portion of them depend on the desire augmentation (EM) calculation. They expect a fundamental likelihood model with boundaries that portray the likelihood as a case that has a place with a certain group. Further, the progressive strategies bunch information occurrences into a tree of bunches. There are two significant strategies under this class. One is the agglomerative technique, which structures the groups in a base up style until all information examples have a place with a similar bunch [14]. The other is the troublesome technique, which partitions the informational index into littler bunches in a top-down style until each group contains just one example.

Both disruptive calculations and agglomerative calculations can be spoken to by dendrograms and are known for their fast end. A couple of instances of various leveled bunching calculations are adjusted iterative lessening and grouping utilizing progressions (BIRCH), bunching utilizing agents (CURE), and CHAMELEON [15]. Thickness-based bunching calculations endeavor to distinguish groups based on the thickness of information focuses in a locale. The key thought of thickness-based bunching is that for each occurrence of a bunch, the area of a given sweep (Eps) must contain at any rate a base number of occurrences (MinPts). A typical thickness-based bunching calculation is the DBSCAN. Grid-based grouping calculations initially quantize the bunching space into a limited number of cells (hyper-square shapes) and afterward perform the necessary procedure on the quantized space [16]. Cells that contain in excess of a specific number of focuses are treated as thick also; the thick cells are associated with structure bunches.

Notable matrix based bunching calculations incorporate the STatistical INformation Matrix based technique (STING), Wave Cluster, and CLustering In QUEst (CLIQUE). Auto-Class depends on the Bayesian methodology. Starting from an arbitrary introduction of the boundaries, it gradually changes them, trying to discover their greatest probability gauges. Further, it is expected that there is a shrouded variable notwithstanding the watched or then again prescient credits [17]. This imperceptibly factor mirrors the bunch participation for each case in the informational index. The data clustering issue is a case of administered gaining from fragmented information because of the presence of such a concealed variable [38]. Their methodology for learning is called recursive Bayesian multinets (RBMNs). A model-based technique is the SOM net, which can be thought of as two layers in a NN. Joining numerous bunching calculations is a more tedious task than joining various classifiers [18]. Bunch groups can be shaped in various ways, for example, the utilization of various diverse bunching methods (either purposely or subjectively chosen), the utilization of a single strategy on various occasions with various starting conditions, and also the utilization of various fractional subsets of highlights or examples. Specify that include choice strategies, such as head segment examination (PCA), straight discriminant investigation, and covering techniques look to diminish the dimensionality of informational collections, distinguish useful highlights, and take out unimportant highlights to abstain from overfitting and underfitting the educated model [19].

4.3   SCOPE OF PATTERN RECOGNITION BY DEEP LEARNING—OVERVIEW

Regardless of the ubiquity of the past strategies, a profound learning insurgency has as of late been abused in a progression of media assignments, for example, sight and sound substance examination and comprehension, recovery, pressure, and transmission, common language preparing (NLP), data recovery, and picture examination [20]. Profound learning alludes to a class of AI that draws strong attention, where layers of data handling stages in progressive structures are misused for design grouping and for highlight or portrayal learning. Three significant purposes behind the notoriety of profound adapting today are definitely expanded chip preparing capacities (for example, GPU units), the fundamentally reduced expense of processing equipment, and late advances in AI and, what is more, benefits in signal-/data-handling research [21].

Convolutional neural networks (CNNs) and their variations have become essential instruments for building profound portrayals to see and comprehend multimodal data, for example, pictures, and also sounds. Be that as it may, because of computational cutoff points, it has not generally been utilized [22]. At the application of the data mining phase, in 1998 analysts applied a slope-based learning calculation to CNNs with victories for the transcribed digit grouping issue. From that point on, CNNs have been improved by a few analysts and accomplished cutting-edge results in various acknowledgment assignments. CNNs are preferred over DNNs for a few reasons,

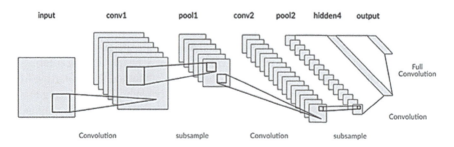

input   conv1   pool1   conv2   pool2   hidden4   output

Full
Convolution

Convolution

Convolution   subsample   Convolution   subsample

FIGURE 4.2   General convolution neural network prototype schema.

including being more like the human visual handling framework, being profoundly upgraded in structure for preparing 2D and 3D pictures, and being viable at learning and extricating deliberations of 2D highlights. Figure 4.2 shows the design of CNNs, which includes two principle parts: highlight extractors and a classifier [23]. In the element extraction layers, each layer of the network gets the yield from the past layer as its information, and furthermore, it passes its yield as the contribution to the following layer. The CNN engineering is a mix of three sorts of layers: convolution, max-pooling, and arrangement.

Repetitive neural networks (RNNs) can be utilized for grouping demonstration and expectation analysis for elevated level semantic information like regular language. In language demonstrating, these organizations endeavor to anticipate the following word or set of words, or certain cases and sentences dependent on past ones. RNNs are networks with circles inside, in this way empowering data to continue [24]. Additionally, RNNs can interface past data to the current task: utilizing past video outlines, understanding present casings, and also endeavoring to create future casings. LSTM models are the most well-known design for worldly data handling.

Lately, motivated by thick convolution, which can secure interpretation invariance, include algorithms that have been adjusted to address point mists characterization and semantic division. These techniques change the inadequate point mists into thick tensors, or concentrate descriptors on the point mists and send these as contribution to DNNs (ConvNets) [25]. Truth be told, learning on a point cloud is troublesome in light of the fact that it is scanty, unstructured, and unordered, and cannot be perceived precisely by a conventional CNN or RNN. Point mists are generally gained by 3D scanners, light recognition and extending (LIDAR), structure-from motion (SFM) methods, and accessible 3D sensors, for example, Kinect and also Xtion. SFM- and photogrammetry-produced point mists normally have a low and inadequate point thickness, while 3D scanners, LIDAR, and profundity sensors can create point mists with additional features [26]. The grouping and semantic division of such information are at present an elevated level errand. Right now, generative models dependent on profound learning have become mainstream and demonstrated extraordinary accomplishment in various application spaces. It is notable that profound learning is an information-driven method that performs better as the quantity of information tests increases. There have been efforts to take care of this issue by creating comparable examples with a generative model. Generative antagonistic organizations (GANs) are an intriguing profound learning approach that was created by Goodfellow in 2014 [27]. GANs are a solo profound learning approach where two NNs go up against one another and every one of the two organizations shows signs of improvement at its given assignment with every cycle. In the instance of the picture age issue, the generator starts with Gaussian clamor to produce pictures and the discriminator decides how great the created pictures are. This cycle proceeds until there are yields for generator advancement. GANs have been utilized to create movement in video, to produce fake video, just as to create point cloud [28].

4.4 TIMES SERIES CLASSIFICATION USING PATTERN CLASSIFICATION

Most of the current strategies for time arrangement grouping work legitimately on time arrangement esteems. Considered are clear time arrangement examinations where information is dissected "with no guarantees". The abundance of calculations devoted to proficient time arrangement handling permitted to lessen the unpredictability of time arrangement similitude assessment by presenting methods, for example, dimensionality decrease and information division or nearby repositories [29]. Taking a look at a wide range of characterization issues, not just in the area of time arrangement examination, one will see that for a programmed design acknowledgment, some of the time it is hard to decide legitimate highlights, for example ,numerically encoded specific properties of a sign, that would accurately segregate between objects that ought to have a place with various gatherings. This is the reason AI puts a high accentuation on the alleged information portrayal, which is the information design on which preparing calculations are dispatched. Conversely to standard example acknowledgment areas, where exchanging information portrayal is a typical practice, existing time arrangement grouping strategies regularly do not present very uncommon changes to information portrayal [30]. The main exceptions are techniques introduced where creators plot time arrangement and convert time arrangement characterization issues to picture acknowledgment issues.

Time arrangement characterization has been seriously explored for well over ten years at this point. Among the mainstream strategies, we find those identified with dynamic time traveling. Dynamic time traveling, DTW for short, is a technique for estimating the likeness between two transient arrangements [31]. It targets coordinating two arrangements in such a way that an expense is limited. The expense is figured as a total of supreme contrasts between the estimations of each pair of coordinated records. Successions are distorted non-directly, which actuates that DTW can be applied to assess the closeness of successions of an alternate length. This is an intriguing notion for how to arrange the time sequence. This strategy, called Move-Split-Merge, depends on the idea that we can change a given time arrangement into some other time arrangement. Steps expected to do this change are named "move" (which changes an estimation of one component), "split" (which changes one component into two sequential components), and "consolidation" (which combines two continuous components into one) [32]. These activities have costs relegated to them (the same in the DTW) and, consequently, the smaller the expense of a change, the more comparative are the double cross arrangements. An unmistakable assortment of techniques targets registering certain factual highlights dependent on time arrangement, for which we wish to process likeness. For instance, there is the idea of a run length of a period arrangement. The referred-to technique includes shaping a histogram of above and beneath the mean run lengths, which guarantees its adaptability to huge informational collections and appropriateness to information streams [33]. Conversely, the ML algorithm splits a period arrangement into various aftereffects, for which certain highlights/designs are processed, and at that point analyzed.

The following overview of strategies proposes the utilization of time arrangement changes. Habitually used changes incorporate shapelets and subordinates. After a period, arrangement informational collection gets changed; one still needs a calculation for assessing closeness [34]. Further, present a technique dependent on numerous changes and a lot of versatile separation measures to ensure strong data fragmentation. It is called COTE, which represents the Group of Transformation-Based Ensembles. To apply time arrangement changes along with the DTW to characterize time intervals. The survey results cover a couple of picture-based techniques for time arrangement. This gathering is small, yet we are recognizing it since the technique discussed in this chapter holds a very high future interpretation in the PR world [35]. The picture-based ways of dealing with time arrangement characterization target encoding time arrangement as pictures. Consequently, a period arrangement characterization issue is changed to a picture acknowledgment issue. By examining a way to deal with time arrangement grouping based on Gramian Angular Summation/Difference Fields and Markov Progress Fields spared as pictures [36]. The initiators of a pattern utilized tiled convolutional neural networks to play out the recent advancement in image processing. Also, encoded time arrangement as Recurrence Plots to find the maximum peak range to fine tune the edge correlations. In these two cases, utilized pictures must be shading or dim scale. Figure 4.3 gives the time series forecasting of a pipeline performance abnormality form pattern classification holding two types of data sets of normal and abnormal [37].

The fundamental issue with the previously mentioned strategies is that the applied picture-based portrayals are "weighty", which requires the discussed portrayals of shading or dim scale plots PR with time arrangement changes the scalar time

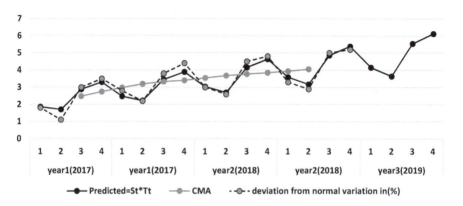

FIGURE 4.3 Pattern classification-based time series forecasting scenario.

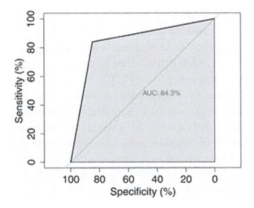

FIGURE 4.4 ROC plot for the pipeline performance using R package.

arrangement into a two-dimensional space of abundancy (time arrangement esteems) and a difference in plentifulness (increase) [38]. Along these lines, the image tuner utilizes this portrayal to plot the information. One figure is delivered for each time arrangement. As a result, the time arrangement order issue is changed into the visual example acknowledgment issue. This change permits the applying of a wide scope of calculations for standard example acknowledgment—in this area, there are a larger number of alternatives to browse than in the space of time arrangement characterization [39].

Further from the time series forecasting graph analysis, we may apply a few visual methods for results review. We have utilized the pROC R bundle to plot receiver operating characteristic (ROC) bends. The bundle smooths the plots to acquire attractive results [40]. A ROC plot presents explicitness against affectability. Figure 4.4 presents the ROC bend for the examined classifier. In light of the state of the bend, we may classify two classes which are perceived with comparative effectiveness and there is no inclination to remember one class better. Extra approval of the ROC is plotting its certainty environments. A certainty span for the ROC curve speaks to the go at a given purpose of explicitness and its relating affectability [41]. Wide spans may recommend issues with the model. This is not the situation in the model that is shown, where we do not see anything disturbing.

4.5 CASE STUDY PATTERN RECOGNITION IN VIDEO SURVEILLANCE FIELD

The advances in PC vision just as AI what is more, profound learning strategies as of late have enhanced the campaign toward reconnaissance; thus, many calculations for the programmed examination of the video arrangements have been proposed. For video observation, AI is generally appropriate in the area of video examination. The value and conceivable outcomes of applying AI to video reconnaissance film are interminable [42]. The clearest advantages would be the capacity for cameras to realize what they are taking a look at and afterward respond to oddities or produce definite reports on the kind of movement they watch. For instance, a camera in a shopping center may give data on what area guests regularly assemble in and could alert security if a group gathers in an area that is normally calm. Information procured through AI in video observation could at last be more important for advertising, and also for operational use than for security [43].

In this way, AI methods have been found to make significant contributions, with a few principle benefits: high exactness and precision in doling out general classes to message information, the capacity to distinguish and imagine discrete designs from a lot of information in situation extraction, and the capacity to make surmises with respect to likely future results in light of models created from existing information [44–49]]. AI calculations have been utilized in three distinct advances: learning the shading change among various cameras, making a more discriminative mark, and tuning the separation metric among tests. Nonetheless, there is incredibly rich data and information implanted in every one of these recordings. With the ongoing advances in PC vision, we can currently mine such enormous visual information to gain important understanding with respect to what is going on, on the planet. Because of the surprising triumphs of profound learning strategies, we can fundamentally support video investigation execution and start new exploration bearings to examine video content [50]. For instance, CNNs have exhibited predominance in displaying significant level visual ideas, while RNNs have appeared guarantee in prioritizing fleeting elements in recordings. Consequently, profound video investigation, or video examination with profound learning, is turning out to be a developing exploration zone in the field of PR [51].

A system for multicamera video observation is proposed that is comprised of three stages: discovery, portrayal, and acknowledgment. The identification stage intertwines video streams from different cameras for removing movement directions from video. The portrayal stage sums up crude direction information to develop progressive, invariant, and substance-rich depictions of movement occasions [52]. Finally, the acknowledgment stage includes occasion arrangement and distinguishes proof of the information descriptors. For successful acknowledgment, they played out a grouping arrangement part capacity to grouping information learning for distinguishing dubious grouping arrangement parts. They indicated that when the positive preparing occasions (i.e., dubious occasions) were dwarfed by the negative preparing examples (kind occasions), at that point SVMs (or some other learning techniques) experienced a high frequency of blunders [53–56]. In order to resolve the existing image processing mechanism, they proposed the piece limit arrangement (KBA) calculation to work with the succession arrangement piece [57].

In another pioneering research study that concentrates on the appearance-based individual acknowledgment which was proposed, pairwise uniqueness profiles (elements of spatial area) between classifications were found to be more adaptive into closes neighbor arrangement [58]. The point was to deal more readily with ambiguities and improve the adaptability of classifiers to a larger number of classifications. To this end, the creators presented a divergence separation measure and straightly or nonlinearly joined it with direct separations. A profound organization engineering was proposed is for passerby data location. Figure 4.5 depicts the contribution of AI

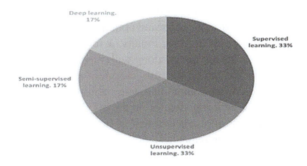

Deep learning. 17%

Supervised learning. 33%

Semi-supervised learning. 17%

Unsupervised learning. 33%

FIGURE 4.5 Contribution of AI in the video surveillance field scenario.

to the field of video surveillance. The application case scenario is well applied in the existing contributions [59].

In their investigation, the pioneering researchers proposed a collaboration between highlight extraction, disfigurement taking care of, impediment taking care of, and order, since these parts are learned and planned separately or successively. They detailed these four parts into a joint profound learning system and proposed a profound organization design [60–62]. The presentation was assessed according to the biggest Caltech benchmark information set. Also, learning approach was proposed for grouping human activities even with no earlier information. The initial step, in view of the augmentation of CNN to 3D, consequently learned spatio-worldly highlights. A RNN was then prepared to arrange each succession by considering the fleeting development of the educated highlights for each time step [63–65]. The investigations were performed on the KTH informational index [66–67].

4.6 CONCLUSIONS

From the developing interest in PC vision methods, it is turning out to be obvious that no single methodology for order is "ideal" and that various strategies and approaches must be utilized. The regular current practice in PR is the blend of a few detecting strategies and classifiers. This chapter provides knowledge on new patterns, procedures, and techniques for PR applied to various fields, and the different PR strategies and applications have been reconsidered. Specifically, a careful study of the literature identified with the utilization of PR and its techniques has been introduced, with a specific consideration of AI and factual and profound learning techniques. PR methods are conveying a promising answer for creating frameworks and empowering the fast-increasing speed of development. The union of PR procedures (machine learning, factual strategy, and profound learning) regarding the nature of information and administrations for genuine applications has three primary parts: wise gadgets, wise arrangement of frameworks, and start-to-finish examination. Further, PR approaches tend toward different difficulties, for example, oddity discovery, multivariate examination, streaming, and perception of data. The broad utilization of PR in various areas has aroused and driven the recognition that such strategies can misuse interactive media information. Encountering difficulties in various areas, the data mining foundations were situated toward obtaining possibilities and frail focuses from a multidisciplinary point of view. Finally, a few fascinating instances of PR applications in various fields are given, along with input design, design classes, and the applied strategy. We are certain that this overview will yield rich data and comprehension of the explored issues identified with the utilization of PR for PC vision applications. Also, it will be instinctive for on the off chance that and how PR strategies and methods can help in the betterment of image processing in the industrial sectors based on the desired prerequisites.

REFERENCES

[1] Ramesh, A. N., Kambhampati, C., Monson, J. R., & Drew, P. J. (2004). Artificial intelligence in medicine. *Annals of the Royal College of Surgeons of England, 86*(5), 334.

[2] Borgia, E. (2014). The internet of things vision: Key features, applications and open issues. *Computer Communications, 54*, 1–31.

[3] Dobre, C., & Xhafa, F. (2014). Intelligent services for big data science. *Future Generation Computer Systems, 37*, 267–281.

[4] Uwah, V., & Ododo, E. (2021). Transformation of instructional process: A review of artificial intelligence in higher institutions. *Asia-Africa Journal of Academic Research and Review, 1*, 63–77.

[5] Gubbi, J., Buyya, R., Marusic, S., & Palaniswami, M. (2013). Internet of Things (IoT): A vision, architectural elements, and future directions. *Future Generation Computer Systems, 29*(7), 1645–1660.

[6] Hollands, R. G. (2015). Critical interventions into the corporate smart city. *Cambridge Journal of Regions, Economy and Society, 8*(1), 61–77.

[7] Ebell, M. H., Rahmatullah, I., Cai, X., Bentivegna, M., Hulme, C., Thompson, M., & Lutz, B. (2021). A systematic review of clinical prediction rules for the diagnosis of influenza. *Journal of the American Board of Family Medicine: JABFM, 34*(6), 1123–1140.

[8] El-Darymli, K., Khan, F., & Mohammed, M.H. (2014). Reliability modeling of wireless sensor networks for oil and gas pipelines monitoring. *Sensors and Transducers Journal, 108*(7), 4122–4133.

[9] Kim, M. (2016) "A quality model for evaluating IoT applications," *International Journal of Computer and Electrical Engineering, 8*(1), 66–70.

[10] Atzori, L., Iera, A., Morabito, G., & Nitti, M. (2012). The Social Internet of Things (SIoT)—when social networks meet the internet of things: concept, architecture and network characterization. *Computer Networks, 56*(16), 3594–3608.

[11] Thillaiarasu, N., & Chenthur Pandian, S. (2019). A novel scheme for safeguarding confidentiality in public clouds for service users of cloud computing. *Cluster Computing, 22*, 1179–1188. https://doi.org/10.1007/s10586-017-1178-8

[12] Latif, S., Driss, M., Boulila, W., e Huma, Z., Jamal, S. S., Idrees, Z., & Ahmad, J. (2021). Deep learning for the Industrial Internet of Things (IIoT): A comprehensive survey of techniques, implementation frameworks, potential applications, and future directions. *Sensors, 21*, 7518.

[13] Ju, G., Cheng, M., Xiao, M., Xu, J., Pan, K., Wang, X., & Shi, F. (2013). Smart transportation between three phases through a stimulus-responsive functionally cooperating device. *Advanced Materials, 25*(21), 2915–2919.

[14] Rehman, M. H., Liew, C. S., Wah, T. Y., Shuja, J., & Daghighi, B. (2015). Mining personal data using smartphones and wearable devices: A survey. *Sensors, 15*, 4430–4469.

[15] Gebhardt, M., Kopyto, M., Birkel, H., & Hartmann, E. (2021). Industry 4.0 technologies as enablers of collaboration in circular supply chains: A systematic literature review. *International Journal of Production Research*, 1–29.

[16] Gevaert, C. M., Carman, M., Rosman, B., Georgiadou, Y., & Soden, R. (2021). Fairness and accountability of AI in disaster risk management: Opportunities and challenges. *Patterns, 2*(11), 100363.

[17] Stokes, K., Castaldo, R., Federici, C., Pagliara, S., Maccaro, A., Cappuccio, F., ... & Pecchia, L. (2022). The use of artificial intelligence systems in diagnosis of pneumonia via signs and symptoms: A systematic review. *Biomedical Signal Processing and Control, 72*, 103325.

[18] Priyanka, E. B., Maheswari, C., & Thangavel, S. (2018). Proactive decision making based IoT framework for an oil pipeline transportation system. In A. Pasumpon Pandian, T. Senjyu, S. M. S. Islam, & H. Wang (Eds.), *Proceeding of the International Conference on Computer Networks, Big Data and IoT (ICCBI – 2018)* (pp. 108–119). Springer, Cham.

[19] Singh, V., Gangsar, P., Porwal, R., & Atulkar, A. (2021). Artificial intelligence application in fault diagnostics of rotating industrial machines: A state-of-the-art review. *Journal of Intelligent Manufacturing*, 1–30.

[20] Chidambaram, S., Sounderajah, V., Maynard, N., & Markar, S. R. (2021). Diagnostic performance of artificial intelligence-centred systems in the diagnosis and postoperative surveillance of upper gastrointestinal malignancies using computed tomography imaging: A systematic review and meta-analysis of diagnostic accuracy. *Annals of Surgical Oncology*, 1–14.

[21] Ozrazgat-Baslanti, T., Loftus, T. J., Ren, Y., Ruppert, M. M., & Bihorac, A. (2021). Advances in artificial intelligence and deep learning systems in ICU-related acute kidney injury. *Current Opinion in Critical Care, 27*(6), 560–572.

[22] Gupta, N., & Jalal, A. S. (2021). Traditional to transfer learning progression on scene text detection and recognition: A survey. *Artificial Intelligence Review*, 1–46.

[23] Garg, M., & Goel, A. (2021). A systematic literature review on online assessment security: Current challenges and integrity strategies. *Computers & Security*, 102544.

[24] Kok, Z. H., Shariff, A. R. M., Alfatni, M. S. M., & Khairunniza-Bejo, S. (2021). Support vector machine in precision agriculture: A review. *Computers and Electronics in Agriculture, 191*, 106546.

[25] Lohrasbinasab, I., Shahraki, A., Taherkordi, A., & Delia Jurcut, A. (2021). From statistical-to machine learning-based network traffic prediction. *Transactions on Emerging Telecommunications Technologies*, e4394.

[26] Rogal, J. (2021). Reaction coordinates in complex systems-a perspective. *The European Physical Journal B, 94*(11), 1–9.

[27] Lin, F., Fang, X., & Gao, Z. (2022). Distributionally robust optimization: A review on theory and applications. *Numerical Algebra, Control & Optimization, 12*(1), 159–212.

[28] Priyanka, E. B., Thangavel, S., & Gao, X. Z. (2021). Review analysis on cloud computing based smart grid technology in the oil pipeline sensor network system. *Petroleum Research, 6*(1), 77–90.

[29] Priyanka, E. B., Thangavel, S., Gao, X. Z., & Sivakumar, N. S. (2021). Digital twin for oil pipeline risk estimation using prognostic and machine learning techniques. *Journal of Industrial Information Integration*, 100272.

[30] Priyanka, E. B., Maheswari, C., & Thangavel, S. (2021). A smart-integrated IoT module for intelligent transportation in oil industry. *International Journal of Numerical Modelling: Electronic Networks, Devices and Fields, 34*(3), e2731.

[31] Den Teuling, N., Pauws, S., & van den Heuvel, E. (2021). Clustering of longitudinal data: A tutorial on a variety of approaches. *arXiv e-prints*, arXiv-2111.

[32] Stokes, K., Castaldo, R., Federici, C., Pagliara, S., Maccaro, A., Cappuccio, F., & Pecchia, L. (2022). The use of artificial intelligence systems in diagnosis of pneumonia via signs and symptoms: A systematic review. *Biomedical Signal Processing and Control, 72*, 103325.

[33] Singh, V., Gangsar, P., Porwal, R., & Atulkar, A. (2021). Artificial intelligence application in fault diagnostics of rotating industrial machines: A state-of-the-art review. *Journal of Intelligent Manufacturing*, 1–30.

[34] Sun, T., Yu, G., Gao, M., Zhao, L., Bai, C., & Yang, W. (2021). Fault diagnosis methods based on machine learning and its applications for wind turbines: A review. *IEEE Access, 9*, 147481–147511.

[35] Amayri, M., Ali, S., Bouguila, N., & Ploix, S. (2021). Machine learning for activity recognition in smart buildings: A survey. In S. Ploix, M. Anayti, & N. Bouguila (Eds.), *Towards Energy Smart Homes* (pp. 199–228). Springer, Cham.

[36] Ali, S., Qaisar, S. B., Saeed, H., Khan, M. F., Naeem, M., & Anpalagan, A. (2015). Network challenges for cyber physical systems with tiny wireless devices: A case study on reliable pipeline condition monitoring. *Sensors, 15*(4), 7172–7205.

[37] Priyanka, E. B., Maheswari, C., Thangavel, S., & Bala, M. P. (2020). Integrating IoT with LQR-PID controller for online surveillance and control of flow and pressure in fluid transportation system. *Journal of Industrial Information Integration, 17*, 100127. https://doi.org/10.1016/j.jii.2020.100127.

[38] Atzori, L., Iera, A., & Morabito, G. (2014). From "smart objects" to "social objects": The next evolutionary step of the internet of things. *IEEE Communications Magazine, 52*(1), 97–105.

[39] Priyanka, E. B., & Thangavel, S. (2020). Influence of Internet of Things (IoT) in association of data mining towards the development smart cities—a review analysis. *Journal of Engineering Science & Technology Review, 13*(4), 1–20.

[40] Priyanka, E. B., Thangavel, S., Meenakshipriya, B., Prabu, D. V., & Sivakumar, N. S. (2021). Big data technologies with computational model computing using hadoop with scheduling challenges. In K. Ahmed & A. E. Hassanien (Eds.), *Deep Learning and Big Data for Intelligent Transportation* (pp. 3–19). Springer, Cham.

[41] Casari, P., Castellani, A. P., Cenedese, A., Lora, C., Rossi, M., Schenato, L., & Zorzi, M. (2009). The wireless sensor networks for city-wide ambient intelligence project. *Sensors, 9*(6), 4056–4082.

[42] Da Xu, L., He, W., & Li, S. (2014). Internet of things in industries: A survey. *IEEE Transactions on Industrial Informatics, 10*(4), 2233–2243.

[43] Terkawi, A., & Innab, N. (2018, April). Major impacts of key reinstallation attack on Internet of Things system. In *2018 21st Saudi Computer Society National Computer Conference (NCC)* (pp. 1–6). IEEE.

[44] Kundu, A., Chaiton, M., Billington, R., Grace, D., Fu, R., Logie, C., ... & Schwartz, R. (2021). Machine learning applications in mental health and substance use research among the LGBTQ2S + population: Scoping review. *JMIR Medical Informatics, 9*(11), e28962.

[45] Li, J., Huang, X., Pianetta, P., & Liu, Y. (2021). Machine-and-data intelligence for synchrotron science. *Nature Reviews Physics, 3*, 766–768.

[46] Preethi, P. et al. An effective digit recognition model using enhanced convolutional neural network based chaotic grey wolf optimization. *Journal of Intelligent & Fuzzy Systems, 41*(2), 3727–3737.

[47] Yan, R., Wang, S., Zhen, L., & Laporte, G. (2021). Emerging approaches applied to maritime transport research: Past and future. *Communications in Transportation Research, 1*, 100011.

[48] Priyanka, E. B., Thangavel, S., Prasad, P. H., & Mohanasundaram, R. (2021). IoT fusion based model predictive pid control approach for oil pipeline infrastructure. *International Journal of Critical Infrastructure Protection, 35*, 100485.

[49] Ponnibala, M., Priyanka, E. B., & Thangavel, S. (2021). Proliferative diabetic retinopathy diagnostic investigation using retinal blood vessels mining technique. *Sensing and Imaging, 22*(1), 1–11.

[50] Priyanka, E. B., & Thangavel, S. (2020, November). Decision making based on machine learning algorithm for identifying failure rates in the oil transportation pipeline. In *2020 International Conference on Decision Sciences and Application (DASA)* (pp. 914–919). IEEE.

[51] Priyanka, E. B., Thangavel, S., Sagayam, K. M., & Elngar, A. A. (2021). Wireless network upgraded with artificial intelligence on the data aggregation towards the smart internet applications. *International Journal of System Assurance Engineering and Management, 13*, 1254–1267.

[52] Priyanka, E. B., Thangavel, S., & Kalavathidevi, T. (2021). Miniaturized antenna design for communication establishment of peer-to-peer communication in the oil pipelines. *Petroleum Research, 6*(3), 291–302.

[53] Zhou, Y., Ge, Y.-T., Shi, X.-L., Wu, K.-Y., Chen, W.-W., Ding, Y.-B., ... & Hu, L.-H. (2021). Machine learning predictive models for acute pancreatitis: A systematic review. *International Journal of Medical Informatics*, 104641.

[54] Nitsche, A. M., Schumann, C. A., Franczyk, B., & Reuther, K. (2021). Mapping supply chain collaboration research: A machine learning-based literature review. *International Journal of Logistics Research and Applications*, 1–29.

[55] Latif, S., Driss, M., Boulila, W., e Huma, Z., Jamal, S. S., Idrees, Z., & Ahmad, J. (2021). Deep learning for the Industrial Internet of Things (IIoT): A comprehensive survey of techniques, implementation frameworks, potential applications, and future directions. *Sensors, 21*, 7518.

[56] Syed, N. F., Shah, S. W., Trujillo-Rasua, R., & Doss, R. (2021). Traceability in supply chains: A cyber security analysis. *Computers & Security*, 102536.

[57] Gómez, Á. L. P., Maimó, L. F., Celdrán, A. H., & Clemente, F. J. G. (2022). Malware detection in industrial scenarios using machine learning and deep learning techniques. In B. B. Gupta (Ed.), *Advances in Malware and Data-Driven Network Security*, 74–93. IGI Global.

[58] Dobrzański, L. A., Dobrzańska, J., Dobrzański, L. B., Dobrzańska-Danikiewicz, A. D., & Gołombek, K. (2021). Development strategy of endodontic filling materials based on engineering and medical approaches. *Processes, 9*(11), 2014.

[59] Gebhardt, M., Kopyto, M., Birkel, H., & Hartmann, E. (2021). Industry 4.0 technologies as enablers of collaboration in circular supply chains: A systematic literature review. *International Journal of Production Research*, 1–29.

[60] De Felice, F., Travaglioni, M., & Petrillo, A. (2021). Innovation trajectories for a Society 5.0. *Data, 6*(11), 115.

[61] Gaikwad, S. R., & Harikrishnan, R. A demand response program for social welfare maximization in the context of the Indian smart grid: A review. In V. Bali, V.

Bhatnagar, D. Aggarwal, S. Bali, & M. J. Diván (Eds.), *Cyber-Physical, IoT, and Autonomous Systems in Industry 4.0*, 25–37. CRC Press.

[62] Bhaskaran, P. E., Chennippan, M., & Subramaniam, T. (2020). Future prediction & estimation of faults occurrences in oil pipelines by using data clustering with time series forecasting. *Journal of Loss Prevention in the Process Industries, 66*, 104203. https://doi.org/10.1016/j.jlp.2020.104203

[63] Priyanka, E. B., Thangavel, S., and Venkatesa Prabu, D. (2020). Fundamentals of Wireless Sensor Networks Using Machine Learning Approaches: Advancement in Big Data Analysis Using Hadoop for Oil Pipeline System With Scheduling Algorithm. In K. M. Sagayam, B. Bhushan. A. D. Andrushia, & V. H. C. de Albuquerque (Eds.), *Deep Learning Strategies for Security Enhancement in Wireless Sensor Networks* (pp. 233–254). IGI Global. https://doi.org/10.4018/978-1-7998-5068-7.ch012

[64] Kim, S. W., Kong, J. H., Lee, S. W., & Lee, S. (2021). Recent advances of artificial intelligence in manufacturing industrial sectors: A review. *International Journal of Precision Engineering and Manufacturing, 23*, 111–129.

[65] Priyanka, E. B., Thangavel, S., & Pratheep, V. G. (2020). Enhanced digital synthesized phase locked loop with high frequency compensation and clock generation. *Sensing and Imaging, 21*(1), 1–12. https://doi.org/10.1007/s11220-020-00308-0

[66] Radoev, M. (2017). A comparison between characteristics of NoSQL databases and traditional databases. *Computer Science and Information Technology, 5*(5), 149–153.

[67] Bhaskaran, P.E., Maheswari, C., Thangavel, S., Ponnibala, M., Kalavathidevi, T., & Sivakumar, N.S. (2021). IoT based monitoring and control of fluid transportation using machine learning. *Computers & Electrical Engineering, 89*, 106899.

Part 2

Industry 4.0

5 A Modified Clonal Selection Algorithm Based on Positive Selection Method in AIS to Solve the Job-Shop Scheduling Problem

R. Murugesan
Department of Mathematics, School of Applied Sciences,
REVA University, Bengaluru, India

CONTENTS

DOI: 10.1201/9781003212201-7

5.1   INTRODUCTION

Scheduling goes hand in hand with planning the assignment of tasks to the available limited resources in any industrial organisation with the purpose of attaining endorsed objectives. Planning specifies an organisation's long-term operations, whereas scheduling directs all the organisation's actions towards completion. Small adjustments in planning and scheduling can have a significant impact on the manufacturing organisation's or industry's overall performance, both in the short and long term. The major performance indicators for the manufacturing industry are resource utilisation, supply chain logistics and inventories, inventory costs, and manufacturing lead times, and meeting due dates, customer satisfaction, quality, variety, and product cost are the primary performance indicators for the manufacturing industry. Figure 5.1 shows the link between planning and scheduling for every activity in the manufacturing industry.

Hence, effective planning and scheduling approaches become essential to develop the performance of manufacturing industries.

Customers drive the global industrial market, since instead of consuming a product made by a manufacturing company, which may differ depending on numerous criteria, such as purpose, lifestyle, and country, they drive the market to manufacture according to their needs. This scenario forces manufacturers to create the same product in a variety of versions and with a variety of facilities. Because the manufacturing business constantly has limited resources, a manufacturer must have effective planning and execution methods to meet customer-oriented market demand. The planning phase generates a blueprint of what to accomplish in order to meet the production criteria, while the execution phase specifies how to put the plan into action. Different departments and levels are involved in the planning and execution.

FIGURE 5.1   Manufacturing environment scheduling.

The production department is one of the most important departments in a manufacturing business. Here, planning determines aspects such as the number of models, the number of products in each model, resource availability, and so on. The number of tasks involved in manufacturing to produce a certain model, the machine eligibility of each duty, the time required for each task on the appropriate machine, the sequencing of tasks on each machine, and so on are all determined by how production and operations are carried out [1]. Each model is referred to as a job in the industry, and the execution procedure is referred to as scheduling. The process of allocating jobs to machines in order to achieve a set of predefined optimality metrics within a set of constraints is called Scheduling. Scheduling difficulties are categorised as "Flow Shop Scheduling (FSS)", "Task Shop Scheduling (JSS)", and "Open Shop Scheduling" (OSS) based on the availability of equipment and the job environment. The Job-Shop Scheduling Problem (JSSP) is a generalisation of all other scheduling issues that affect the majority of manufacturing sectors. The solution methodology for addressing JSSP using artificial intelligence is discussed in this chapter.

Today's manufacturing industries engage in mass production to be highly competitive in the global market. The size and complexity of scheduling problems are increased in mass production. This leads to the scheduling problem becoming a non-polynomial (NP) hard optimisation problem. Traditional methodologies [1–7] either take a long time to find the best solution or fail when the problem gets non-polynomial (NP) hard. As a result, it becomes even more critical to develop effective, best, and rapid planning and scheduling solutions for resolving such scheduling issues. The heuristic-based algorithms [3, 5, 7–14] such as "Genetic Algorithms", "Neural Networks", "Particle Swarm Optimisation", "Ant Colony Optimisation", "Tabu search", "Simulated annealing", and, more recently, "Artificial Immune System" (AIS)-based algorithms have all been considered for developing such techniques. AIS-based algorithms, such as combinatorial JSSP, FSS, OSS, and others, are frequently employed due to their adaptive nature in behaviour for varied applications with a wide variety of problem sizes. The AIS algorithm was created using bio immune system theoretical immunology, immune functionals, concepts, and types of models [2, 11]. Also, the applications [15, 16] of AIS are computer security and network security, fault and anomaly detection, data analysis, and data mining optimisation computation.

Learning ability, memory of the occurrence, and strongness of the insusceptible framework make it great for taking care of booking issues "[17]". An AIS-based counterfeit insightful technique for addressing JSSP begins with the suspicion that ideal arrangements exist in the arrangement space. The calculations' motivation is to utilise both neighbourhood search and worldwide hunt techniques to decide the ideal arrangement. The arrangement space for the JSSP with N number of occupations and M number of machines is the most extreme number of arrangements of $(N!)M$, that is, an issue planned with 10 positions and 10 machines (10X10) and it has $(10!)10= 3.9594e+065$ potential arrangements. Identifying all possible arrangements to find the best one is unreasonable. Thus, a decrease in the arrangement search space from absolute space becomes basic [18]. This should be possible by either beginning the hunt from a superior spot or utilising a directed arrangement space search. In this review, the AIS is utilised to give a directed pursuit strategy. This part is coordinated as follows: the issue articulation, the AIS for tackling JSSP, the PSMCSA calculation, execution measure, mathematical assessment, assessment of the PSMCSA calculation, and the end.

5.2 JOB-SHOP SCHEDULING PROBLEM

The JSSP comprises N number of occupations (i.e. $j = 1,2,...,N$) that should be handled on M number of machines (i.e. $I = 1,2,...,M$) while sticking to the accompanying rules. There is no machine distribution for occupations since they are developed of activities, $O_j = O_{1j} O_{2j}, ..., O_{mj}$ (O-activity). Each activity ought to be handled on every single machine. Each machine is fit for dealing with just each occupation in turn. Each activity makes some handling memories p_{ij} and a beginning time r_{ij}. As indicated by a mechanical course, every activity of a particular occupation should be handled after its archetype P_{ij} and before its replacement S_{ij}. This part examines finding an ideal timetable fully intent on limiting the makes pan with least time length and creating an enormous number of ideal timetables for an evolving climate.

5.3 ARTIFICIAL IMMUNE SYSTEM (AIS)

The bio insusceptible framework rouses the Artificial Immune System (AIS) [5, 11,15, 16, 19–21].

The bio insusceptible framework, which watches one's body, assaults irresistible sicknesses like microscopic organisms and infections. Any microbe that the resistant framework can perceive, is called an antigen. The insusceptible framework responds with a certain goal in mind when an antigen is found. T and B lymphocytes are particular cells in our invulnerable framework that assume a huge part. Both B-cells and T-cells have receptor particles that permit them to perceive explicit targets. Immune system microorganisms do not distinguish a "non-self" target, like a microbe, unless antigens (little parts of the microorganism) are handled and furnished related to a "self" receptor known as the significant histocompatibility complex (MHC) atom. Executioner T-cells and assistant T-cells are two sorts of T-cells. Antigens associated with Class I MHC atoms must be distinguished by aide T-cells, while antigens connected to Class II MHC particles must be perceived by executioner T-cells. These two antigen methods address the jobs of the two sorts of T-cells. Assistant T-cells are answerable for both intrinsic and versatile safe reactions, just like the body's invulnerable reaction to a particular infection. These cells do not obliterate or eliminate microbes from contaminated cells nearby. All things considered, they direct the resistant reaction by advising different cells to do their jobs, for example, executioner T-cells and B-cells. The B-cell, then again, is an antigen-explicit receptor that can perceive entire contaminations without processing them. The total scope of B-cell antigen receptors represents the whole scope of antibodies that the body might deliver, on the grounds that every B-cell ancestry communicates an alternate immuniser. Antibodies on a B-surface cell perceive a particular unfamiliar antigen as a microorganism when they tie to it. The antigen/neutraliser mix is consumed by the B-cell and changed over to peptides by proteolysis [22–46]. These antigenic peptides are then shown on the MHC class II particles of the B-surface cell. This

MHC and antigen mix draws in a coordinating with a partner T-cell, which discharges lymphokines and actuates the B-cell. The offspring of an actuated B-cell (plasma cells) makes a large number of duplicates of the antigen-perceiving counteracting agent as B-cell partitions. These antibodies flow in the blood plasma and lymph, append to antigen-creating microorganisms, and name them for supplement actuation or phagocyte retention obliteration.

Antibodies can likewise straightforwardly handle risks by restricting bacterial poisons or meddling with infections and microbe-tainting cell receptors. A portion of the descendants of actuated B-cells and T-cells convert into enduring memory cells when they start repeating. These memory cells recollect every individual micro-organism that a natural experiences during its life and can mount a vigorous reaction assuming the contamination is recognised once more. This is alluded to as "versatile" nature since it happens during an individual's life as a response to contamination with that microbe and readies a safe framework for future difficulties. Inactive transient memory and dynamic long haul memory are two kinds of immunological memory. Antibodies and antigens are significant pieces of the AIS of the bio resistant frame-work. Both the counteracting agent and antigen can be addressed and decoded simi-larly for the given climate.

5.3.1 Positive Selection Theory

Genes are the fundamental components of antibodies and antigens. They are made up of a string of multiple genes. T-cell receptors are similar to B-cell receptors in that they do not secrete antibodies and do not bind directly to antigens. They instead attach to peptides (small fragments of pathogen protein) that are provided in a com-pound with a specialised self-molecule (MHC). MHC is a specialised complex that regulates the immune system's T-cell response. The widely held belief is that the diversity in MHC between individuals ensures that everyone's immune system does not react to infections in the same way. Positive selection is an area in immunology where there are contrasting views. The ability of positive and negative selects to work together to keep cells that recognise the self-MHC peptide complex while eliminating cells that recognise any self-peptides is at issue.

5.3.2 Clonal Selection Theory

The body has a large number of particular lymphocytes, which express a great many various receptors with changing specificities, the number of which is known as the singular's receptor collection. This collection is exposed to a choice component during the singular's life expectancy to give a versatile resistant reaction. Burnet (1959) proposed the clonal choice hypothesis to clarify how an adequate number of lymphocytes equipped for identifying a particular sickness may be made to assault it. This hypothesis was created when there was little but some familiarity with lympho-cyte action and the state of their receptors; however, it has been displayed to chip away at both B and T cells. Immunology has become viewed as the investigation of self or non-self-separation since it has turned into an essential standard of versatile resistance. The idea suggests that when enough antigen ties, lymphocytes become enacted. At the point when a lymphocyte is initiated, it produces clones with the very receptors as the first cell that got the antigen. Subsequently, the underlying lymphocyte goes through clonal multiplication.

According to Janeway et al. (2001), the four essential concepts of clonal selection are the following:

1 Every lymphocyte has just one sort of receptor with its very own explicitness.
2 Lymphocytic initiation happens when an unfamiliar particle cooperates with a lymphocyte equipped for restricting that atom with a high partiality.
3 Separated effector cells created from actuated lymphocytes will have receptors with similar explicitness as the parental cells from which they were shaped.
4 Lymphocytes with receptors for pervasive self-particles are wiped out from the get-go in lymphoid cell improvement and thus do not show up in the collection of mature lymphocytes. Clonal erasure is the third of these standards.

It stops lymphocyte receptors that are made arbitrarily from distinguishing the body's own tissue particles and setting off a safe reaction against them (Janeway et al. 2001). The clonal choice hypothesis is summed up in Figure 5.2. Burnet (1959) introduced the express idea that subatomic material is either important for a person or not in immunology with the foundation of the clonal determination hypothesis and its essentialness for clonal erasure (Tauber 2000). Accordingly, one of the invulnerable framework's essential capacities has turned into the grouping of antigens as one or the other self or non-self. To achieve this qualification, no self-responding lymphocytes should be available in the collection. Along these lines, any antigen that responds with a lymphocyte receptor should be non-self and ought to be erased.

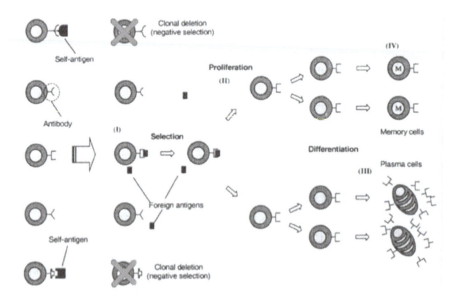

FIGURE 5.2 The theory clonal selection, negative selection, proliferation and differentiation (de Castro and Timmis).

Despite the fact that it was just a hypothesis at that point, clonal erasure was subsequently found to exist in the body through a component known as bad determination, which works on lymphocytes during their development. This happens to T-cells in the thymus, which has a great deal of APCs that current self-antigens. Youthful T-cells that cling to these self-antigens forcefully pass on in a controlled way (apoptosis). Therefore, T-cells that endure this stage ought to be safe to self-antigens. Immunological resistance alludes to lymphocytes' capacity to not respond to themselves (de Castro and Timmis 2002a).

5.3.3 AFFINITY MATURATION

Various changes have been made to the first clonal choice theory since it was created to incorporate later exploratory outcomes. One such finding was that during B-cell clonal turn of event (yet not T-cell clonal development), the normal neutraliser fondness for the antigen that set off the clonal extension expanded. The term for this peculiarity is partiality development. Because of the more noteworthy liking of the counteracting agent for the antigen, the insusceptible reaction is more proficient after future antigen openness. During the clonal expansion of B-cells, a physical hypermutation and choice instrument cause proclivity development. Counteracting agent explicitness is changed by physical hypermutation, which acquaints irregular modifications with the qualities that code for their V areas. This hyper-transformation system is believed to be relative to antigen-immune response restricting fondness, implying that the more grounded the counteracting agent partiality, the fewer changes it encounters. Following the changes, the B-cells that produce higher liking antibodies are specially chosen to form into effector and memory cells, bringing about an increment in the normal populace proclivity of antibodies throughout the span of a safe reaction (Goldsby et al. 2003, de Castro and Timmis 2002b).

5.4 REPRESENTATION OF JSSP IN AIS

Fake Immune System is shown to be exceptionally versatile, as other naturally roused methods, appropriate for number of utilisations could be viewed as a clever delicate registering worldview, ideal for reconciliation with a lot more customary procedures (de Castro and Timmis 2003). CSA is shown to be more applicable for dealing with planning issues among the recognised AIS-based strategies like the Clonal Selection Algorithm (CSA), Negative Selection Algorithm, Artificial Immune Network, and Danger Theory. This has been made possible by populace-based working systems, self-association, learning, memory, and versatility to the climate, in addition to other things. In any case, a number of scholars, including Dasgupta and Aickelin, have commented that AIS-based calculations sometimes fall short for all sort and size difficulties. Accordingly, various analysts in the field of booking have fostered a mix of AIS with different strategies/calculations like the Genetic Algorithm, Particle Optimisation Algorithm, Tabu Search, Ant Colony Optimisation, and so on. This section aims to consolidate the CSA not with different methodologies but rather with AIS's own components. The CSA depends on the B-cell instrument in the bio-safe framework. Immune system microorganisms, then again, behave as energisers for

B-cells, making them perceive antigen and start the B-cell process. Immune system microorganism development is joined with CSA in this investigation. As a precursor to this inquiry, a comprehensive report and investigation of the CSA-based computation for settling JSSP is made. This examination sets the street for recognising the hole and creating ways to deal with further development of CSA. This part goes through every one of these exhaustively, just as the PSMCSA calculation.

Antigen and immuniser are expected to address the ideal and potential timetables separately, to make the similarity between invulnerable framework and JSSP more self-evident. The CSA creates a lot of antibodies that cover every one of the likely timetables for the thought about Job Shop scheduling problem (JSSP). A timetable is an answer to the workshop booking issue, which is characterised as JxM activities of J occupations on M machines in an assembling climate. Every activity has a set handling time, and each occupation has a cut-off time by which it should be finished; this is steady across all analyses. A machine can just deal with each occupation in turn, and no procedure on any machine can be pre-empted. There is a particular appearance date for every task. The expense of a timetable straightforwardly corresponds to the culmination season of the last errand, and the nature of a timetable is evaluated by makes pan, given the finish of handling season of occupations on each machine.

5.4.1 Shape-Space Model of AIS for JSSP

The goal of the shape-space model is to produce a quantitative representation of antigen-antibody interactions (Ag-Ab). The generalised shape of a molecule refers to the set of characteristics that define it. The binary or real-valued Ag-Ab representation provides a distance measure that may be used to calculate the degree of contact between these molecules. A set of coordinate vectors $Ab = <Ab_1, Ab_2, ..., Ab_N>$ can be treated as a point in an N-dimensional real-valued shape-space ($Ab \cdot S^N$) to describe the generalised shape of a molecule, whether an antibody or an antigen. The exact physical meaning of each parameter is not important for the construction of computational tools, but it is important for the problem at hand. Potential schedules based on the shape-space model, as well as the best schedule achieved at that time instant, are used as antibodies (Ab) and antigens (Ag) in this study. Antibodies (Ab) and antigens (Ag) with the same length L are represented as integer strings. The length is determined by the magnitude of the challenge and how the cells are represented. A potential schedule in JSSP is a set of jobs in the processing machines or a set of tasks in the processing machines. A schedule, Ab and Ag, has the same length in both circumstances, which is equal to the product of the number of jobs and machines. Because the eligibility of a machine to process a job is predefined, a schedule is represented in this study as a sequence of jobs in the order in which they would be considered for processing in the production shop. As a result, a machine cannot require a job for processing, as well as a preferred job sequence as a schedule. When a JSSP has J jobs and M machines, the length of the schedule L is equal to JxM. In addition to the description of length, the representation of an antibody/schedule should be defined. An antibody/schedule is represented as an integer string, where each integer represents a job number, which is repeated by the number of machine times.

A job's task number is determined by the number of times it occurs.

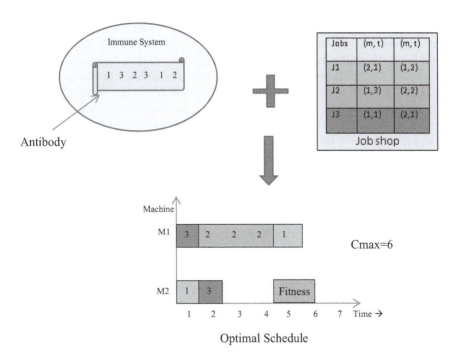

FIGURE 5.3 Operation of AIS for solving JSSP.

In Figure 5.3, these representations, as well as the role of AIS in the production of JSSP schedules, are depicted graphically.

5.4.2 COMPONENTS IN CSA FOR JSSP REPRESENTATION

Counteracting agent – Antibody expresses that the cells inside the body, like T-cells and B-cells, that battle against sickness or infection contaminate it in hypothetical immunology. A neutraliser is a likely arrangement with regards to booking, for example, potential timetables that might be ideal timetables produced by a calculation. Since it resolves the central concern, it is named an immuniser. These timetables will then, at that point, be investigated to check whether they are the most productive as far as the makespan. Neutraliser libraries are utilised to make antibodies.

Counteracting agent Library – To shield self-tissues from antigens, the human invulnerable framework relies upon B-cells and T-cells in the human body. Antigens do not have a specific design or creation since they adjust to their environmental elements and take on different shapes to install themselves in the body. B-cells should create antibodies with, however, many unmistakable shapes and constructions as can be expected under the circumstances to battle these numerous shapes and structures and to shield the body. The safe framework, then again, has a set number of changes. There are strings of B-cells that join and develop the most confounded designs to keep the safe framework equipped for engaging potential contaminations. This arrangement of lines of B-cells is called an antibody library. Subsequently, when a contamination strikes, the resistant framework looks for a particular blend of variables that will permit it to defeat the danger. Essentially, a counterfeit insusceptible framework follows a similar thought for a similar motivation to have the option to be used for a wide scope of issues while at the same time being sufficiently adaptable to react to changes inside the issue. One of the essential elements of AIS, especially in CSA, is the idea of libraries that put away the strings or portions of arrangements, like timetables, which might be connected to different libraries through an assortment of stages and mixes. As far as JSSP, a counteracting agent library is an assortment of inadequate timetables. It fundamentally comprises strings (or segments) of timetables that, when associated together, make a total timetable.

Chromosome – Each immuniser library has chromosomes, which are an assortment of parts. In science, every chromosome has its own properties. A chromosome in the JSSP scientific classification will demonstrate either a task arrangement in a specific machine or a machine grouping for a particular assignment, or it very well may be an activity succession including various positions that are interrelated and happen habitually in a creation shop. In an immuniser, the quantity of chromosomes and the length of every chromosome are client characterised boundaries. These boundaries can be set before the immuniser is fabricated. Antibodies are worked out of a blend of chromosomes from different libraries.

Qualities – A quality is the least difficult and most fundamental part of a counteracting agent. An immuniser library's chromosome is comprised of a gathering of qualities. In JSSP, a quality is an essential activity unit of a task or assignment that will be handled by a machine until it is finished without being pre-empted. In JSSP, the quantity of libraries, chromosomes, and qualities in the test shifts, relying upon the number of occupations and machines included. The length of quality is the quantity of qualities in a solitary counteracting agent and is equivalent to the number of occupations increase with the number of machines. Along these lines a six work and six machines issue would have 36 qualities all out. In a safe framework, an antigen library is an assortment of antibodies that have been picked as the arrangement from a gathering of antibodies. In JSSP, an antigen library includes a lot of potential timetables for a specific creation shop set-up. An antigen library's all out number of antigens that can be kept, is prefixed. Assuming another immuniser or timetable has the smallest makespan of any antigen or plan for the library, that counteracting agent is enlisted as an antigen and will supplant the antigen with the longest makespan (or least worth) in the library. The method involved with making antibodies/plans, surveying them, and picking better timetables for the antigen library is rehashed however many occasions as the mentioned number of emphases or until the necessary timetables are made.

5.4.3 Clonal Selection Algorithm for JSSP

In the wake of concentrating on the clonal determination rule and the proclivity development process, making the CSA is basic. The vitally safe perspectives thought about were choice and cloning of the most animated cells, fondness development and re-choice of the clones with higher partiality, hypermutation relative to cell liking, memory cells practically detached from the collection, demise of non-invigorated cells, and age and support of variety. In the calculation, the counteracting agent is an applicant plan, though the antigen is a contender plan that will be the best timetable created at that point.

The algorithm works as follows.

5.4.3.1   Basic Clonal Selection Algorithm (CLONALG) for Solving JSSP

1. Create a set (P) of potential schedules that will be accommodated as the initial antibody population.
2. In the first generation, evaluate the affinity f (makespan) of antibodies.
3. Form a cloned population for each antibody by generating n_c clones of each antibody. n_c is the number of clones of an antibody that can be computed based on its affinity.
4. Each cloned population is subjected to a hypermutation method in which the hypermutation is proportionate to the antibody's affinity. It creates a matured cloned population (C*).
5. By rejecting other clones, choose the best clone from C* to replace its parent's position in the new population. The new population is viewed as a potential contender for the following generation.

This method repeats as many times as specified or until the best environmental solution is found. The optimum solution is the best schedule for the JSSP in question, which will achieve optimal or near-optimal results by meeting the predetermined restrictions. In the next sections, each of the processes in this operational mechanism is detailed in depth, along with the findings for an example benchmark JSSP. Figure 5.5 depicts the algorithm's flow chart, whereas Figure 5.4 depicts the realisation pseudo code.

5.4.3.2   Cloning Operation in CSA

Cloning is the process of multiplying antibodies chosen by Positive Selection Algorithms (PSAs) and populating them in the first generation of an antigen library, and the following equation calculates the number of clones produced by antibody "i":

$$n_i = ceil\left(N^c \left(\frac{f(x_i)}{\sum_{i=1}^{N} f(x_i)} \right) \right), \tag{5.1}$$

where N^c is a predetermined value for the cloning rates, ceil (.) is defined as the operator that rounds its input to the next larger integer, and $f(x_i)$ measures the fitness of an antibody i. Clearly, the stronger the affinity, the greater the number of copies, and vice versa.

5.4.3.3   Mutation Schemes in CSA for JSSP

The CSA mutation operation is used in JSSP to improve the local search mechanism, which will help speed up the algorithm's convergence and increase the variety of the

Define Antigen Generation buffer A Gi=1with the buffer size N
Populate Gi =1 with the selected antibodies by the positive selection
algorithm

Define Cloned Generation buffer CGi=1with the buffer size N populated with
zeros

> *Start for loop i from 1 to NG number of generation*
> *Start for loop k from 1 to NA number of antibodies*
> > *Read antibody k from AGi*
> > *Generate Nik number of clones A1ik of antibody Aik and*
> > > *buffered in CGi*
> > *Mutate A1ik and calculate affinity*
> > *Select the best antibody from mutated A1ik and buffered in*
> > > *CGi*

> *End for k one generation*

*/***** steps for improving AGi using CGi*

> *Sort CGi with respect to affinity*
> *Compare AGi and CGi and replace swap the better antibodies to AGi*
> *from CGi*

End for i

FIGURE 5.4   Implementation of the basic clonal selection algorithm (CLONALG).

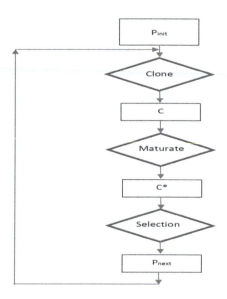

FIGURE 5.5   Flow chart of clonal selection algorithm.

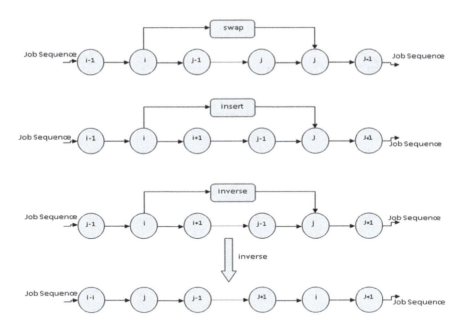

FIGURE 5.6   Local search operations in JSSP.

solution population. The change of work sequence in a single machine or between several machines is viewed as a mutation in the JSSP solution. As a result, in JSSP, single-point mutation is preferred. To improve the variety of the solution (antibody library) population and improve the quality of the solution, three types of single-point mutations are used in this study: insertion, transposition, and inversion (Figures 5.6a and b).

Figure 5.6 The three mutation operations.

Transposition mutation: pick two places at random from a job permutation and swap them.

Insertion mutation: pick two alternative sites at random from a job permutation and insert the rear one first.

Inversion mutation is the inverse of a job permutation's subsequence between two separate random places.

Genes are switched in their positions in Figure 5.7, a single-point transposition mutation. Figure 5.7 depicts a transposition mutation with two different mutations: A1 is called the parent antibody, and A1' is called the offspring generated by swapping genes 5 and 6, and 1 and 2. The offspring A1' is an insertion of 5 and 1 between 3 and 6, and 5 and 3 of the parent antibodies in insertion. A1' is a transposition of genes 3 and 3 of its parent antibody in inversion.

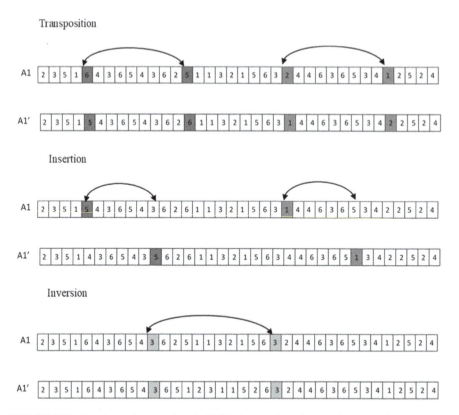

FIGURE 5.7 Local search operations in JSSP via mutation of an antibody in CSA.

5.4.4　MODIFICATION REQUIREMENT IN THE CLONAL SELECTION ALGORITHM

In the present CSA, the library of next-generation antibodies is chosen from the cloned version of the current-generation library without considering the parent library, as shown in the Figure 5.7. During this screening process, there is a possibility of missing the superior antibodies from the parent collection. Generating cloned antibodies with higher affinity for an optimum solution may not be guaranteed with the higher mutation rate. As a result, it is suggested that the current clonal selection procedure be changed. The two modifications are as follows:

1. Before selecting the next-generation antigen library, the parent antibody library is concatenated with the cloned and modified antibody libraries. This will prevent a single parent antibody from producing a large number of superior antibodies. Because of this alteration, the algorithm is forced to find the best answer in the first iteration.
2. New algorithm termination criteria are proposed, requiring the algorithm to search for several optimal solutions for a certain number of runs even if it

finds the best answer early on. As a result, the algorithm generates a solid solution library with a number of excellent options. This adjustment is most advantageous in the changing environment of the current situation.

5.4.4.1 Positive Selection-based Modified Clonal Selection Algorithm (PSMCSA)

The recommended solution approach for solving JSSP has two parts. To populate the CSA's first-generation population, the first step uses a T-cell-based PSA. In most cases, a random population or chaotic operation is used to initialise the system. The PSA selects the most effective antibodies for the creation of an antigen library, which is subsequently transmitted to the second stage. In the second stage of the algorithm, the final solution library (FSL) is generated for the given problem using a Modified Clonal Selection Algorithm (MCSA). This newly proposed algorithm is named Positive Selection-based Modified Clonal Selection Algorithm (PSMCSA). The newly proposed algorithm is detailed in the following section.

5.4.4.2 M1: Building an Antibody from an Antibody Library

An antibody is created from chromosomes, and the genes of chromosomes represent a schedule of machines to jobs and they must be processed in a specific order. The technique for creating such an antibody would be as follows:

1. Pick a library at random.
2. Pick a chromosome randomly from the selected library.
3. Copy the selected chromosome into the antibody.
4. Pick a different library at random (a library once selected cannot be selected again).
5. Pick randomly a chromosome and concatenate it with the antibody from a point after the end of the previous chromosome.
6. Repeat the steps 4 and 5 until the antibody is completely filled.

A sample antibody generation is detailed in Figure 5.8.

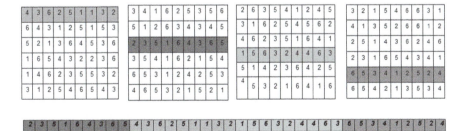

FIGURE 5.8 Antibody generation from a set of chromosome libraries.

5.4.4.3   Positive Selection in AIS

Positive selection is derived from the maturation mechanism of T-cells in the immune system, just as clonal selection comes from the maturation mechanism of B-cells in the human immune system. Helper cells, killer cells, alpha cells, and other types of T-cells exist in the bio immune system. In the immune system, each cell has a distinct purpose. T-cells are involved in the front layer of the immune system, where they help the B-cells identify antigens in the body and attack by killing them, as well as assist the B-cells in identifying antigens in the body by stimulating the matching B-cells for stronger and longer protection against the same antigens. Because the B-cell-based CSA includes all of the mechanisms required for solving engineering computational problems. Moreover, the notion of positive selection mechanism has had the least progress and the most disagreements within the bio immune system research society, PSA has failed to pique the interest of engineers. Nonetheless, in the AIS, F. Celada and P. E. Seiden introduced the positive selection-based approach.

The PSA is developed based on the human immune system. This algorithm selects the antibodies that are beneficial in combating illness. Similarly, the algorithm looks for antibodies that have the potential to help with the JSS challenge. In order to recognise possibly suitable schedules, a threshold is defined for makespan values and those schedules that pose the makespan lower than the threshold are retained in the system, while the rest are rejected. Threshold is a predetermined value that defines the boundary between good and bad solutions.

M2: Positive Selection Algorithm in AIS

In AIS, the PSA picks antibodies with higher affinity than the affinity measure parameter's fixed threshold. The affinity threshold is preserved as the fitness threshold in a manufacturing facility since it determines the fitness of the schedules for a certain JSSP.

The minimal makespan (Cmax), that is, min.Cmax, is used to set this fitness threshold. The antibodies chosen by the PSA with respect to this defined fitness threshold are advanced to the next level of AIS. Figure 5.9 shows the processing steps in the PSA.

The fitness value and the objective function for a solution of JSSP are defined as follows:

$$Fitness = \left(Max\left(C_{ij}\right)\right); \qquad \forall i \in \{i:1-N\}; \ \forall j \in \{j:1-M\} \qquad (5.2)$$

$$Objective = min\left(Max\left(C_{ij}\right)\right); \qquad \forall i \in \{i:1-N\}; \ \forall j \in \{j:1-M\} \qquad (5.3)$$

The initial antibody library is populated using antibodies created from the antibody libraries in this algorithm. Antibody libraries, as described in the previous section of this chapter, are filled with partial or entire schedules, which are identical to chromosomes and antibodies, respectively. The created schedule is tested for the makespan after each antibody is decoded into a schedule for the given problem.

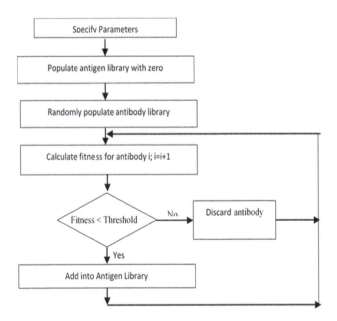

FIGURE 5.9   Flow diagram for positive selection algorithm.

Fitness is calculated for each antibody and compared to the threshold. If an antibody's fitness falls below the threshold level, it is deemed a potential schedule and is moved on to the next stage of processing; otherwise, it is discarded.

5.4.4.4   M3: Modified Clonal Selection Algorithm

The following are proposed changes to the present CSA:

1. Improved Clonal Selection Algorithm initiation by employing an immune system-inspired positive selection method to begin the search for the best solution from a better starting point.
2. Effective mutation using the log-normal mutation operator with a fixed mutation rate and the coefficient of restitution (COR) mutation operator with an adaptive mutation rate
3. Receptor editing based on a society: Creating an antibody society from antigen families prior to receptor editing. This will prevent the production of many superior antibodies from a single antigen. This change forces the algorithm to find the best answer in the first runs.
4. Modified algorithm termination criteria. That is, the search for optimal solutions is continued for the predetermined number of runs even if an optimal solution is arrived at the earlier runs.

As a result, the algorithm creates a robust solution library containing several ideal solutions.

The implementation steps in PSMCSA are as follows:

1. Define the antigen library (AGL) with N number of antigens.
2. Define the cloned antibody library (CAL) with NC sizes such that NC = N*nc, where nc is the number of clones created for each antigen in the AGL. nc is a constant in this proposed algorithm.
3. Combined clonal library (CCL) of size NC+N is created.
4. Load the antigen library generated by PSA into the first generation of AGLrk (r:1-R; k:1-K). R is the number of runs in the algorithm and K is the number of generations in a run.
5. Fill zeros in the first cloned antibody library, CALk.
6. In AGLrk (r = 1 and k = 1), create nc niches for each antigen. For agirkAGLrk, for example, a set agijrkagi1rk,agi2rk, agi3rk... agincrk is created.
7. Make niches that are not what they used to be.
8. Use agijrk to populate CALk.
9. Assess the antibodies' fitness in CALk
10. Combine CALk and AGLrk to create CCLk and their respective fitness libraries.
11. Sort the antibodies by their fitness in increasing order.
12. AGLrk receptor editing, that is, selecting N antibodies from CCLk that occupy the top N positions and populating AGLrk. Then multiply AGLrk by AGLrk+1.
13. Examine the scheduling problem's terminating criteria. If they are met, stop the operation; otherwise, proceed to step 4 to generate antigen clones in AGLrk+1. Operation Stop indicates the end of the algorithm.
14. The final AGLrk | k=K provides the set of best solutions at the end of a single run of the proposed algorithm.
15. Repeat steps from 1 to 10 for several runs, with the final results of each run being added to the FSL. There could be a number of optimal solutions in this FSL. For the given situation, the best option is chosen from the FSL.

Figure 5.10 shows the flow chart of the PSMCSA

5.4.4.5   M4: Evolutionary Mutation in CSA

In detecting the mutating locations, the mutation algorithms differ. Here, two distinct mutation algorithms are studied, both of which are based on evolutionary algorithms. By increasing diversity amongst solutions in solution libraries, evolutionary algorithms introduce the self-adaptive potential to avoid local optima. The first algorithm is the normal mutation operator (NMO), in which the mutating points are recognised by normal distributed numbers, and the second algorithm is the log-normal mutation operator (LNMO), in which the same is identified by the log-normal distribution. The self-adaptively log-normal mutation operator is incorporated into the algorithm to increase the likelihood of jumping out of the local optimum.

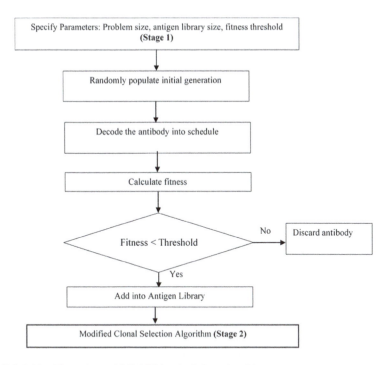

FIGURE 5.10   Flow chart of PSMCSA scheduling algorithm.

Each clone, save the parent, undergoes self-adaptive mutation according to the following formula:

Each parent $\left(x_i,\ \sigma_i\right)$, $\forall i \in 1,\ 2,\ldots \mu, create a single off-spring\left(x_i',\ \sigma_i'\right) by$:

$$\sigma_i'(j) = \sigma_i(j) e^{\left(\alpha N(0,1) + \beta N_j(0,1)\right)} x_j'(j) = x_i(j)\sigma_i'(j)\beta N_j(0,1) \qquad (5.4)$$

where $x_i(j)$, $x_i'(j)$, $\sigma_i(j)$, $\sigma_i'(j)$ denote the *jth* component of the vectors *xi, xi', σi, and σi'* respectively *for j=1,.,.,.n,*. $N_j(0,\ 1)$ is a normally distributed one-dimensional random number with zero as the mean and one as the standard deviation. $N_j(0,1)$ is a new random number which is generated for every *j*. The factors α and β are commonly set to 1/sqrt (2sqrt(*n*)) and 1/(2sqrt(*n*)) respectively. In a normal mutation operator, the mutating point is updated by normal distributed σ instead of log-normal σ.

5.4.5   REALISATION OF THE **PSMCSA** ALGORITHM

The suggested PSMCSA technique is implemented in MATLAB to investigate performance and is tested using the OR library's JSSP benchmark examples. This section contains a step-by-step realisation procedure as well as a sample result for FT06. Table 5.1 shows a problem JSSP with six jobs with six operations in each job and six

TABLE 5.1
JSSP FT06

Jobs	m,t	m,t	m,t	m,t	m,t	m,t
1	3,1	1,3	2,6	4,7	6,3	5,6
2	2,8	3,5	5,10	6,10	1,10	4,4
3	3,5	4,4	6,8	1,9	2,1	5,7
4	2,5	1,5	3,5	4,3	5,8	6,9
5	3,9	2,3	5,5	6,4	1,3	4,1
6	2,3	4,3	6,9	1,10	5,4	3,1

TABLE 5.2
Sample of Simulation Parameters for Studying the PSMCSA Algorithm

S.NO	Parameters	Values
1	Initial Population Size	100
2	Makespan threshold for PSA	70
3	Antigen library size	N = 5 (for an instance)
4	Number of clones per antigen	$n_c = 100$
5	Number of mutations per antibody	Mu = 12 points
6	Antibody generation size	$NC = N*n_c = 500$
7	Number of generation per iteration	K = 10
8	Number of iterations	M = 10
9	Final solution library size	N*M = 50

machines for processing jobs. Table 5.1 shows the machine allocation and processing time on the allotted machine for each operation of a job.

5.4.5.1 AIS Parameters Selection for Solving JSSP

Fixing the AIS parameters for the proposed algorithm is the primary priority in the realisation. Certain parameters must be set up at the start of the process, while others can be set up later. The size of the antigen library and the fitness threshold of the PSA are two factors that must be selected at the start of the process. Values of parameters like the number of modified niches per antibody, mutations per clone in the clonal selection method, and the size of the FSL can be determined later in the algorithm. The parameters of the suggested method are chosen through trial and error, which can result in superior outcomes in terms of both solution quality and computing time. The algorithm parameters chosen for researching FT06 are listed in Table 5.2. These criteria will vary depending on the size and difficulty of the task.

5.4.6 GENERATION OF AN ANTIGEN LIBRARY FROM THE PSA

In the initial population, there are 100 antibodies. This population is derived from the antibody library, as detailed in the section "4.6.1 M1: Antibody Library Construction."

6	5	3	1	4	2	2	4	1	6	3	5	4	5	2	6	3	1	6	4	3	5	1	2	5	4	3	6	2	1	3	6	1	4	5	2
4	3	2	5	6	1	2	3	5	1	4	6	5	1	2	4	3	6	1	5	4	2	3	6	4	2	1	3	6	5	6	2	3	1	4	5
3	6	2	4	5	1	1	3	4	6	2	5	5	3	4	6	1	2	1	5	6	2	3	4	6	1	4	2	5	3	2	3	4	5	6	1
4	3	6	5	1	2	1	5	6	4	2	3	6	3	2	5	4	1	2	5	1	4	6	3	2	6	3	1	5	4	2	4	6	3	1	5
6	5	2	3	1	4	2	1	3	5	6	4	4	2	3	1	6	5	3	4	2	1	5	6	4	2	1	6	5	3	3	2	5	6	1	4

FIGURE 5.11 Sample library with a set of antigens.

59	60	61	61	62

FIGURE 5.12 Makespan of antigen library generated by PSA.

6	5	3	1	4	2	2	4	1	6	3	5	4	5	2	6	3	1	6	4	3	5	1	2	5	4	3	6	2	1	3	6	1	4	5	2
6	5	3	1	4	2	2	4	1	6	3	5	4	5	2	6	3	1	6	4	3	5	1	2	5	4	3	6	2	1	3	6	1	4	5	2
6	5	3	1	4	2	2	4	1	6	3	5	4	5	2	6	3	1	6	4	3	5	1	2	5	4	3	6	2	1	3	6	1	4	5	2
6	5	3	1	4	2	2	4	1	6	3	5	4	5	2	6	3	1	6	4	3	5	1	2	5	4	3	6	2	1	3	6	1	4	5	2
6	5	3	1	4	2	2	4	1	6	3	5	4	5	2	6	3	1	6	4	3	5	1	2	5	4	3	6	2	1	3	6	1	4	5	2

FIGURE 5.13 Cloning set of antigen 1 in the antigen library.

59	59	59	59	59

FIGURE 5.14 Makespan of clones.

The PSA selects an antigen library from this starting population using a predetermined fitness threshold of 70. Minimum and maximum values of makespan are 68 and 118 respectively. The PSA chooses the top five antigens based on the pre-set threshold value of 70. Figure 5.11 shows one antigen library with five antigens and Figure 5.12 shows their corresponding makespan. Antigens selected by the PSA are given to the next stage. Cloning and hyper mutation are performed on each antigen.

The chosen antigen library is used as the initial population in the PSMCSA algorithm's second stage, from which the FSL is generated. Modified CSA in the second stage creates 100 clones or antibodies for each antigen and adds them to the current generation's cloned antibody library. Figures 5.13 and 5.14 show a partial cloning set containing five clones for the first antigen from the antigen library, as well as their makespan. The log-normal mutation approach is used to mutate these antibodies.

Figure 5.15 lists the modified antibodies, while Figure 5.16 lists their corresponding makespan. The parent antigen has a 59-year lifespan. The makespan of the mutant antibodies ranges from 59 to 115. The goal of the log-normal mutation operator is to get out of the local optima, as evidenced by the significant variation of makespan. Table 5.3 and Figure 5.17, which exhibit the distribution metrics of the solution

6	5	3	1	4	2	2	4	1	6	3	5	4	5	2	6	3	1	6	4	3	5	1	2	5	4	3	6	2	1	3	6	1	4	5	2
6	1	3	1	4	2	2	4	5	6	3	5	4	5	2	6	6	1	3	4	3	6	1	2	5	4	6	3	2	4	3	5	1	1	5	2
6	5	3	3	2	2	6	4	1	6	1	5	4	5	4	4	3	2	6	6	3	5	1	2	5	4	3	2	2	1	3	6	1	4	5	1
6	5	3	5	6	2	2	4	1	4	3	5	4	5	2	2	3	6	6	6	3	1	1	2	5	4	3	1	2	1	3	4	1	4	5	6
6	5	3	1	1	4	5	4	1	6	3	5	4	6	1	5	5	1	6	2	3	2	1	2	5	4	3	6	2	2	3	6	4	4	3	2

FIGURE 5.15   Mutation with 12 points.

59	80	85	115	74

FIGURE 5.16   Makespan of first generation of antigen 1.

TABLE 5.3
Performance Measure of Evolutionary Mutation

Performance parameters	Initial Library	GMO	LMNO
GD (mean)	2.9193	4.2911	4.3114
GD (std)	1.0122	1.5145	1.5243
S(mean)	3.3800e-013	3.2384e-009	3.5919e-009
S(std)	2.9617e-013	5.0860e-009	5.9828e-009

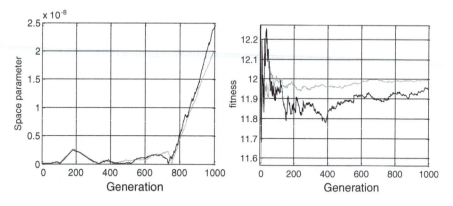

FIGURE 5.17   Fitness and distribution of solutions in JSSP due to MMO and LNMO.

population and the distribution of fitness parameters for the JSSP FT06 under consideration, better illustrate the property of the log-normal mutation operator.

All other antigens' cloning and modified antibodies libraries are merged with the mutated cloning library. In the algorithm, this merged library is referred to as the global library. The global library is first decrypted, then assessed, and then sorted. The top five antibodies are chosen from this sorted global library and promoted to the

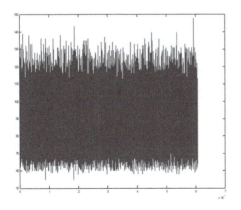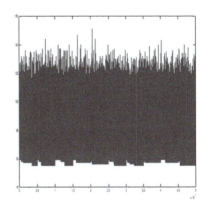

FIGURE 5.18 Makespan generated over 10 generations: a) CLONALG; b) PSMCSA.

TABLE 5.4
Average Makespan Variation over 10 Iterations of CLONALG Population

| Generation | Makespan Variation of Individuals in Antigen Library | | | | |
	Antigen 1	Antigen 2	Antigen 3	Antigen 4	Antigen 5
1	81.10	80.89	82.21	81.15	81.69
2	80.64	80.51	80.66	80.77	81.99
3	81.55	81.21	80.47	80.24	82.35
4	80.28	80.83	79.89	79.72	79.99
5	79.87	80.03	81.26	80.69	82.02
6	80.15	80.06	80.44	81.29	80.79
7	80.17	80.37	81.35	81.41	81.59
8	80.50	81.24	80.54	80.71	81.21
9	79.44	79.39	80.31	80.52	79.54
10	80.52	80.73	81.40	79.73	79.93

next generation as the initial population antigen library. This process is repeated for a fixed number of iterations. In the given example, the complete process was performed for ten generations per iteration to ensure that the optimum result was repeatable. For ten iterations, the produced global libraries are accumulated. Figure 5.18 shows the variation of makespan of each member of the accumulated library. The CLONALG algorithm-generated graph is shown in a, while the proposed PSMCSA algorithm-generated graph is shown in b. The figure clearly illustrates that the suggested method produces the best schedules for practically all generation types and achieves the best results in all iterations. It is also discovered that there are numerous unique optimal solutions. In a single iteration, these optimal solutions developed over ten generations form the FSL.

Tables 5.4 and 5.6 show the fluctuation of the makespan in one of the iterations for CLONALG and PSMCSA, respectively. Tables 5.5 and 5.7 show the FSL generated

TABLE 5.5

Minimum Makespan of Individual Antigen in CLONALG FSL

	Minimum Makespan Variation of Individuals in CLONALG FSL				
Generation	Antigen 1	Antigen 2	Antigen 3	Antigen 4	Antigen 5
1	61	59	60	59	61
2	61	58	59	59	60
3	60	58	59	59	59
4	58	56	59	59	58
5	58	56	59	59	58
6	58	56	59	59	58
7	58	56	59	59	58
8	58	55	59	59	58
9	58	55	59	57	58
10	58	55	59	57	57

TABLE 5.6

Average Makespan Variation over 10 Iterations of PSMCSA Population

	Makespan Variation of Individuals in Antigen Library				
Generation	Antigen 1	Antigen 2	Antigen 3	Antigen 4	Antigen 5
1	79.64	82.42	79.70	81.09	81.64
2	79.55	80.16	79.86	81.50	82.54
3	77.94	80.44	79.61	81.99	80.22
4	80.49	80.57	79.34	79.22	79.85
5	80.46	79.38	79.27	78.25	79.33
6	81.15	80.44	82.55	78.37	78.84
7	80.20	81.79	83.50	80.44	80.03
8	80.01	81.29	83.88	81.87	80.71
9	79.11	79.92	83.53	81.53	80.32
10	79.36	80.21	82.91	80.44	80.34

by CLONALG and PSMCSA, respectively. Tables indicate that the PSAMCSA significantly outperforms CLONALG in terms of number of optimal solutions in the FSL. In comparison to CLONALG's three ideal solutions, PSMCSA generated 30 optimal solutions. Figure 5.19 shows the partial FSL generated by PSMCSA. The ideal schedules for five antibodies for FT06 are listed in this table, each with a makespan of 55. Table 5.8 shows FSL's performance metrics. For the same initial population, PSMCSA provides superior diversity and space metrics over CLONALG, as well as a robustness of 56.5 in contrast to 60.6 for CLONALG. Chapter 5 contains a full performance analysis of PSMCSA for various sizes and complicated problems from the OR library, as well as other performance measures.

TABLE 5.7
Minimum makespan of individual antigen in PSMCSA FSL

Generation	Minimum Makespan Variation of Individuals in PSMCSA FSL				
	Antigen 1	Antigen 2	Antigen 3	Antigen 4	Antigen 5
1	59	60	61	61	62
2	58	59	59	60	61
3	57	58	58	58	58
4	55	56	57	55	58
5	55	56	55	55	56
6	55	55	55	55	55
7	55	55	55	55	55
8	55	55	55	55	55
9	55	55	55	55	55
10	55	55	55	55	55

3	2	1	3	4	4	2	3	6	5	6	4	4	5	3	2	3	6	5	4	2	1	5	6	3	1	2	1	6	1	1	2	6	5	5	4
3	2	1	3	3	1	2	4	6	5	6	1	1	2	6	4	3	6	5	5	2	3	5	4	2	3	4	1	5	4	4	2	5	6	6	1
2	3	1	3	4	6	2	2	4	5	6	4	5	5	3	3	3	4	4	6	1	2	5	6	3	1	2	1	6	1	1	2	6	5	5	4
2	3	1	3	4	1	2	2	3	5	6	5	4	5	4	6	3	4	6	4	1	2	5	3	3	6	2	1	6	1	1	2	6	5	5	4
2	3	4	6	1	3	2	2	1	5	6	4	3	5	3	6	3	4	4	6	1	2	5	3	5	4	2	1	6	1	1	2	6	5	5	4

FIGURE 5.19 Part of final solution library having makespan = 55 (optimal schedules).

TABLE 5.8
Performance Characteristics of FSL

Performance parameters	CLONALG	PSMCSA
GD (mean)	2.9193	4.3114
GD (std)	1.0122	1.5243
S(mean)	3.3800e-013	1.419e-07
S(std)	2.9617e-013	5.983e-07
Mean of Cmax	60.6	55.5

5.5 CONCLUSION

The positive selection-based PSMCSA algorithm is proposed in this chapter to improve the basic performance of the CSA. The main benefit of the PSA in this method is that it gives the instances a better starting position. Furthermore, for all instances of the same sort of JSSP in terms of number of jobs and machines, a single pool of antibodies (100 antibodies) is used to generate an antigen library. This chapter provides a step-by-step walkthrough of the realisation process of the proposed algorithm. The traditional Clonal Selection Algorithm (CLONALG) is also implemented in MATLAB® to demonstrate the differences in realisation and performance. FSL was not created in the original CLONALG proposed by E. Hart. This chapter has incorporated it as a point of reference. The newly proposed algorithm generates a FSL with numerous optimal schedules which can be used as a solution methodology for solving various JSSP in a changing environment without changes in job readiness sequence or permanent failure of machines.

REFERENCES

1. B. Giffler and G.L. Thompson. Algorithms for Solving Production Scheduling Problems, *Operations Research*, Vol. 8(4), 1960, pp. 487–503.
2. C. Rego and R. Duarte. A Filter-And-Fan Approach to the Job Shop Scheduling Problem. *European Journal of Operational Research*, Vol. 194, 2009, pp. 650662.
3. C. Y. Zhang, P. Li, and Z. Guan. A Very Fast TS/SA Algorithm for the Job Shop Scheduling Problem. *Computers & Operations Research*, Vol. 35, 2008, pp. 282–294.
4. H. Chiu, K. Hsieh, Y. T. Tang, and W. Chien. Employing a Genetic Algorithm Based on Knowledge to Address the Job Shop Scheduling Problem. *WSEAS Transaction on Computer Research*, Vol. 2, Issue 2, February 2007, pp. 327–333.
5. N. Thillaiarasu, N. Gowthaman, and S. Chenthur Pandian. Design of a Confidentiality Model Using Semantic-Based Information Segmentation (SBIS) and Scattered Storage in Cloud Computing. In S. Nath Sur, V. E. Balas, A. K. Bhoi, and A. Nayyar (eds.) *IoT and IoE Driven Smart Cities*. EAI/Springer Innovations in Communication and Computing. Springer, Cham, 2022. https://doi.org/10.1007/978-3-030-82715-1_9
6. N. Thillaiarasu, S. C. Pandian, and N. Gowthaman (2022) Novel Heuristic Scheme to Enforce Safety and Confidentiality Using Feature-Based Encryption in Multi-cloud Environment (MCE). In T. Guarda, S. Anwar, M. Leon, and F. J. Mota Pinto (eds.) *Information and Knowledge in Internet of Things*. EAI/Springer Innovations in Communication and Computing. Springer, Cham, 2022. https://doi.org/10.1007/978-3-030-75123-4_20
7. P. Preethi et al. An Effective Digit Recognition Model Using Enhanced Convolutional Neural Network Based Chaotic Grey Wolf Optimization. *Journal of Intelligent & Fuzzy Systems*, Vol. 41, No. 2, 2021, pp. 3727–3737.
8. F. Croce, R. Tadei, and G. Volta. A Genetic Algorithm for the Job Shop Problem. *Computers and Operations Research*, Vol. 22, No. 1, 1995, pp. 15–24.
9. D. Y. Sha and C. Hsu. A Hybrid Particle Swarm Optimization for Job Shop Scheduling Problem. *Computers & Industrial Engineering*, Vol. 51, No. 4, 2006, pp. 791–808.
10. H. R. Lourenco. Local Optimization and the Job Shop Scheduling Problem. *European Journal of Operational Research*, Vol. 83, 1995, pp. 347–364.
11. N. Thillaiarasu, S. C. Pandian, V. Vijayakumar et al. Designing a trivial information relaying scheme for assuring safety in mobile cloud computing environment. *Wireless Networks*, Vol. 27, 2021, pp. 5477–5490. https://doi.org/10.1007/s11276-019-02113-4
12. L. Wang, and D. Zheng, An Effective Hybrid Optimisation Strategy for Job-Shop Scheduling Problems. *Computers & Operations Research*, Vol. 28, 2001, pp. 585–596.

13. M. L. Pinedo. *Planning and Scheduling in Manufacturing and Services*. Series in Operations Research and Financial Engineering. Springer Verlag, 2006.

14. Jiaquan Gao and Jun Wang. WBMOAIS: A Novel Artificial Immune System for Multiobjective Optimization. *Computers& Operation Research*, Vol. 37, No. 1, 2010, pp. 50–61.

15. D. Dasgupta and F. Gonzalez. Artificial Immune Systems (AIS) Research in the Last Five Years. In *Proceedings of Conference Evolutionary Computation*, 2003, pp. 123–130.

16. L. N. De Castro, and J. Timmis. *Artificial Immune Systems: A New Computational Intelligence Paradigm*. London, 2002: Springer-Verlag.

17. E. Nowicki and C. Smutnicki. A Fast Taboo Search Algorithm for the Job Shop Problem. *Management Science*, Vol. 42, No. 6, 1996, pp. 797–813.

18. E. Hart and P. Ross. An Immune System Approach to Scheduling in Changing Environments. GECCO'99. https://dl.acm.org/doi/10.5555/2934046.2934157

19. P. Malini, N. Gowthaman, A. Gautami, and N. Thillaiarasu. Internet of Everything (IoE) in Smart City Paradigm Using Advanced Sensors for Handheld Devices and Equipment. In S. Nath Sur, V. E. Balas, A. K. Bhoi, and A. Nayyar (eds.) *IoT and IoE Driven Smart Cities*. EAI/Springer Innovations in Communication and Computing. Springer, Cham, 2022. https://doi.org/10.1007/978-3-030-82715-1_6

20. J. Carlier and E. Pinson. A Practical Use of Jackson's Preemptive Schedule for Solving the Job Shop Problem. *Annals of Operations Research*, Vol. 26, 1990, pp. 269–287.

21. N. Shyamambika and N. Thillaiarasu. A Survey on Acquiring Integrity of Shared Data with Effective User Termination in the Cloud. *2016 10th International Conference on Intelligent Systems and Control (ISCO)*, 2016, pp. 1–5. https://doi.org/10.1109/ISCO.2016.7726893.

22. Carlos A. Coello, Daniel Cortes Rivera, and Nareli Cruz Cortes. Use of an Artificial Immune System for Job Shop Scheduling. In *Proceeding of Second International Conference on Artificial Immune Systems (ICARIS)*, September 1–3, 2003, Napier University, Edinburgh, UK.

23. E.H.L. Aarts, P.J.M. Van Laarhoven, J.K. Lenstra, and N.L.J. Ulder. A Computational Study of Local Search Algorithms for Job Shop Scheduling. *ORSA Journal on Computing*, Vol. 6, 1994, pp. 118–125.

24. F. Celada and P. E. Seiden. Modeling Immune Cognition. In *Proceedings of the IEEE International Conference on Systems, Man, and Cybernetics*, 11–14 October, 1998. IEEE.

25. F. Celada and P. E. Seiden. Affinity Maturation and Hypermutation in a Simulation of the Humoral Immune Response. *European Journal of Immunology* , Vol. 26, 1996, pp. 1350–1358.

26. W. Q. Huang and A. H. Yin. An Improved Shifting Bottleneck Procedure for the Job Shop Scheduling Problem. *Computers & Operations Research*, 2004. www.sciencedirect.com/science/article/abs/pii/S030505480300243

27. H. Zhou, Y. Feng, and L. Han, The Hybrid Heuristic Genetic Algorithm for Job Shop Scheduling. *Computers & Industrial Engineering*, Vol. 40, 2001, pp. 191–200.

28. Y. Mati Essafi and S. D. Peres. A Genetic Local Search Algorithm for Minimizing Total Weighted Tardiness in the Job-Shop Scheduling Problem. *Computers & Operations Research*, Vol. 35, Issue 8, 2008, pp. 2599–2616.

29. R. Murugesan and K. Sivasakthi Balan. Clonal Selection Algorithm Using Improved Initialization for Solving JSSP.

30. J. F. Gonzalves, J. M. Mendes, and M. C. G. Resende. A Hybrid Genetic Algorithm for the Job Shop Scheduling Problem. *European Journal of Operational Research*, Vol. 167, 2005, pp. 77–95.

31. K. Mori, M. Tsukiyama, and T. Fukuda. Adaptive Scheduling System Inspired by Immune System. In *SMC'98 Conference Proceedings. 1998 IEEE International Conference on Systems, Man, and Cybernetics*, 1998, Vol. 4, pp. 3833–3837. IEEE.

32. N. Thillaiarasu and S. Chenthur Pandian. A Novel Scheme for Safeguarding Confidentiality in Public Clouds for Service Users of Cloud Computing. *Cluster Computing*, Vol. 22, pp. 1179–1188, 2019. https://doi.org/10.1007/s10586-017-1178-8

33. N. Thillaiarasu and S. Chenthur Pandian, Enforcing Security and Privacy over Multi-Cloud Framework Using Assessment Techniques. *2016 10th International Conference on Intelligent Systems and Control (ISCO)*, 2016, pp. 1–5. https://doi.org./10.1109/ISCO.2016.7727001.

34. N. Shyamambika and N. Thillaiarasu. Attaining Integrity, Secured Data Sharing and Removal of Misbehaving Client in the Public Cloud Using an External Agent and Secure Encryption Technique. *Advances in Natural and Applied Sciences*, Vol. 10, No. 9 SE, 2016, pp. 421–432.

35. R. Murugesan and V. Navaneetha Kumar. A Fast Algorithm for Solving JSSP. *European Journal of Scientific Research*, Vol. 64, No. 4, 2011, pp. 579–586.

36. R. Murugesan, and K. Sivasakthi Balan. Positive Selection Based Modified Clonal Selection Algorithm for Solving Job Shop Scheduling Problem. *Applied Mathematical Sciences*, Vol. 6, No. 46, 2012, pp. 2255–2271.

37. Leandro Nunes de Castro and Fernando J. Von Zuben. The Clonal Selection Algorithm with Engineering Applications. *Workshop Proceedings of GECCO*, 2000, pp. 36. https://citeseerx.ist.psu.edu/viewdoc/download?doi=10.1.1.25.6636&rep=rep1&type=pdf

38. R. Murugesan. Novel Method for Performance Measure of Job Shop Scheduling Algorithm. *International Journal of Computational and Applied Mathematics*, Vol. 8, No. 4, 2013, pp. 285–295.

39. Leandro Nunes de Castro and Fernando Jose Von Zuben. *Artificial Immune System: Part I Basic Theory and Applications*. Technical Report, TRDCA 01/99

40. R. Murugesan, K. S. Balan, and V. N. Kumar. Clonal Selection Algorithm Using Improved Initialization for Solving JSSP. *2010 International Conference on Communication Control and Computing Technologies (ICCCCT)*, 2010, pp. 470–475.

41. R. Murugesan and V. Navaneethakumar. A Fast Algorithm for Solving Job Shop Scheduling Using Artificial Immune System. *European Journal of Scientific Research*, Vol. 64, No. 4, 2011, pp. 579–586.

42. P. Brucker, B. Jurisch, and B. Sievers. A Branch and Bound Algorithm for Job-Shop Scheduling Problem. *Discrete Applied Mathematics*, Vol. 49, 1994, pp. 105–127.

43. R. M. Aiex, S. Binato, and M. G. C. Resende. Parallel GRASP with Path Relinking for Job Shop Scheduling. *Parallel Computing*, Vol. 29, No. 4, 2003, pp. 393–430.

44. T. Fukuda, K. Mori, and M. Tsukiyama. Immune Networks Using Genetic Algorithm for Adaptive Production Scheduling. In *15th IFAC World Congress*, Vol. 3, pp. 57–60, 1993.

45. U. Dorndorf and E. Pesch. Evolution Based Learning in a Job Shop Environment. *Computers and Operations Research*, Vol. 22, 1995, pp. 25–40.

46. Leandro Nunes de Castro and Fernando Jose Von Zuben. *Artificial Immune System: Part I Basic Theory and Applications*. Technical Report, TR DCA 01/99.

6 IoT Health Care Devices for Patient Monitoring

N. Palanivel, P. Sathiyanarayanan, R. Indumathi, and V. Selvi
Department of CSE, Manakula Vinayagar Institute of
Technology, Puducherry, India

CONTENTS

6.1 INTRODUCTION

The well-being area is growing admirably and has wide possibilities. This progression depends on the utilization of development and the utilization of the Internet of Things (IoT) trap. It consolidates the advancement of data and correspondence (IoT), the utilization of sensors, the period of gigantic data and the utilization of enormous data, man-made brainpower and man-made reasoning cycles. The utilization of the most recent developments is especially appropriate for long-haul treatment of patients with flow illnesses [1], the number of which has as of late expanded. Developments in the Internet of Things (IoT) give new responses to diabetic patients

Constant infections are depicted as long haul and require long-haul treatment. Patients with steady diseases for the most part spend quite a while in a clinical center for nonstop checking. Some constant potential diseases are normal, for example, coronary illness or diabetes. Diabetes is as of now risky in light of the fact that it causes numerous infections consistently. Thus, patients with diabetes should be checked to live an ordinary life. Diabetes might be a persistent crack of the pancreas, which happens when the pancreas cannot give the right degree of insulin or the body cannot utilize insulin appropriately [1]. High or low glucose levels can harm and debilitate numerous organs, like the eyes, nerves, and veins; subsequently, consistent every day checking is important to avoid the loss of strength of diabetic patients. Given the number of diabetic patients, more structures are expected to screen these patients. The diabetes checking structure centers around normal blood glucose observing. This implies that patients, relatives and medical services experts can rapidly screen blood glucose levels whenever necessary. Compact portable diabetes screens enjoy numerous benefits, including improving the existence of diabetic patients using far-off inventive innovation, which has an astonishing capacity to pass on understanding data to specialists.

In light of this, the fifth-generation (5G) advancement, known as the period of cutting-edge wearable associations, can accomplish quick exchange, development of big business limits and hierarchical versatility. Be that as it may, the current assessment of this development centers around growing the data submitted [2]. In this chapter, we advance a plan for persistent and complex perceptions of diabetic patients that utilize artificial intelligence (AI) estimations to sort out data. Our proposed configuration incorporates all-inclusive sensors for determining the patient's blood glucose level, temperature and dynamic work. The cell phone sends the data gathered by the sensor to the account station through the 5G cell network association. The information gathered and examined incorporates introductions. Furthermore, gauge through some question computations of diabetics clinical analysts.

6.2   RELATED WORK

This section analyzes composed surveys of certain references identified with convenient applications that utilize AI figuring to screen diabetic patients. The plan of the proposed structure is introduced, and consequently, the estimations utilized in this study are presented. Canny designing is used for recognizing diabetes contaminations and to measure the strength of diabetic patients using sensors installed in phones [3–7]. Another study utilized Hadoop to plan and compute decay, snare assumptions and treatment-type assumptions [8], to inspect the visualization of diabetes types, and the maker of [9] proposed a design that fulfills mellitus' assumptions, a disease in which the body does not control the amount of glucose (a type of sugar) in the blood and the kidneys make a large amount of urine.

On the off-chance that a patient uses Hadoop/Map Reduce, this might be some kind of diabetes. The glucose strategy is proposed in [10]. The data produced by ceaseless blood glucose checking is decayed by glucoSim programming utilizing Kalman channel (KF) to decrease commotion. Examiners utilize diverse data handling strategies to make and carry out various confirmation and assumption models. In [11], the maker utilized a gathering technique with guileless Bayesian computations and a choice tree with Weka instruments to look for plans from the diabetes data set. In [12], the maker utilized innocent Bayesian techniques and choice trees in a solitary model cluster to check covered-up structures in the diabetes data set.

Self-administration by diabetic patients is constrained by specialist patient communication. The communication is brought out through a global system for mobile communication, a sensor is associated with n cell phones, and the patient value is transferred to the distributed storage. The specialist will momentarily present the patient with an eating regimen, a workout and so on. The chapter authors recommend utilizing Bluetooth to trade patient readings with associated gadgets. In any case, we suggest utilizing Universal Asynchronous Receiver/Transmitter (UART) to gather raspberry readings. Pi is a basic method to share information. The authors have set up a GSM organization to transfer information to the cloud. We use Wi-Fi for download meetings to guarantee quick information transmission between sender and collector. We have tracked down a superior arrangement. Give a predictable, protected, consistent and pervasive foundation for IoT patient screens. The Internet of Things is utilized for voice identification, internal heat level, electrocardiogram and natural stickiness.

Controlling glucose can help an individual keep their glucose levels within a specific objective reach through a reasonable eating regimen, exercise and insulin, all of which can decrease the chance of diabetes difficulties. There are many verifying instruments that can help individuals control diabetes. This chapter gives a framework that can screen patients' blood glucose levels and store them in the cloud. Both patients and specialists can obtain current and authentic information to arrive at better medication and nourishing choices.

6.3   PROPOSED SYSTEM

This part gives a total portrayal of the proposed 5G diabetes executives framework. The goal of this chapter is to use 5G technology to convey data and AI to monitor diabetes patients' blood glucose levels for data the executives and assembling. The advancement to foster a complex 5G structure for consistent checking of diabetic patients is accomplished through a progression of sensors, wearable gadgets, versatile applications and informational index laborers, which are utilized in mechanical design. From one viewpoint, Wi-Fi is utilized to interface various sensors to the telephone. Conversely, 5G advancement is utilized to associate cell phones to cell organizations to send data to informational indexes. It was determined that the proposed design can gather data about the glucose level, temperature and genuine examination of diabetic patients, and afterward utilize the cell phone to send information by blending 5G with the base station. The system then utilizes computerized reasoning and man-made consciousness procedures to brilliantly control information to assist clients with accomplishing objective glucose levels and anticipating future well-being changes

A patient's glucose level, when there are small changes in the level, does not imply that the patient's condition is deteriorating under normal conditions. Nevertheless, consistent pressure can show amazing outcomes, for example, outrageous Kussmaul sluggishness, visual weakness and even demise. As per reports, diabetics ordinarily follow a diabetes treatment plan that is based on the suggestion to take insulin routinely. At the point when patients misconceived quality, experts got stunning news. Based on this information, specialists can recommend explicit measures to address this issue. Cells are denser and more moderate in 5G associations, and they provide astonishingly high transmission speeds to client associations.

As a feature of the further advancement of the 5G association, these gadgets have various qualities. Additionally, good wishes. Being astute about one's health

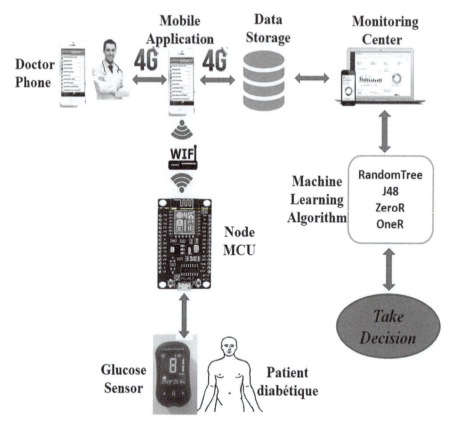

FIGURE 6.1   Proposed system.

necessitates using the right sensors and technology to generate the various types of data. The right preparation and utilization of this data require different kinds of authoritative advantages, like flexibility, responsibility, security, vital control, steady quality and the gradualness of observing well-being components. Patients must keep in contact with their primary care physician. Patients are not required to be examined wherever they are. 5G is utilized in some well-being applications.

Quite possibly the most broadly utilized advance is the tangible emotionally supportive network for observing diabetic patients, which deals with the onboarding of new individuals, diabetic patients, relatives or others who have been inspired by the illness. The client should complete the enrollment structure (Figure 6.1). They utilize their own data and pick a username and secret key for the record. After gathering data and effectively signing up, clients can sign in and utilize the chance of various administrations. The client profile entered during enrollment should be overseen. It is imperative to naturally record sensor readings. The sensor should be associated with the diabetic patient, and the radio-frequency identification (RFID) tag should be associated with the patient's hand.

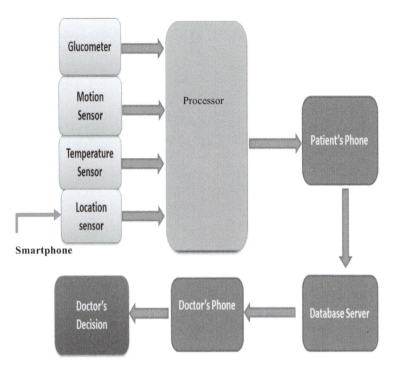

FIGURE 6.2   Hardware block diagram.

6.3.1   HARDWARE COMPONENTS AND WORKING PRINCIPLE

In this undertaking we decided to assess the glucose level, thump, heartbeat and temperature. The glucose sensor, circulatory strain and temperature sensor, and beat sensor are connected to the Arduino nano Analogue to Digital Converter (ADC) (Figure 6.2). The Arduino nano relate through the USB interface with the Raspberry Pi. The Raspberry Pi is connected with the cloud through Wi-Fi.

6.3.2   SENSORS

Here, we present the details of the sensors we have used in our project.

a)   One-Touch Glucose Monitor

A one-touch glucose monitor is not hard to utilize. It has sound alarms with hiding and sound cautions. It is a real-time product. In this study we utilized it for glucose checking by get its essential attributes (Figure 6.3). We utilize this one-touch persistent thing to obtain the glucose level of the patients. We get the direct unit and force supply beginning there we get the simple to state of the art worth by Arduino nano.

FIGURE 6.3   One-touch glucose monitor.

FIGURE 6.4   Pulse sensor.

b)   Pulse Sensor

The pulse sensor assesses the adjustment of blood volume going through any organ of the body depending on the light body diagram standard, which will cause an adjustment of the force of light going (Figure 6.4) through that organ (vascular region), that is, the patient's pulse. Infrared light sensor.

c)   Temperature and Blood Pressure Sensor

A crushing element sensor is a device that dedects pressing part and converts it into a fundamental electric sign whose size is determined by the crushing element used. Since they convert pressure into an electrical sign, they are also named crushing element transducers (Figure 6.5). A temperature sensor is a combined circuit that can intertwine wide sign dealing with hardware inside a close pack as the sensor. There is no compelling reason to include pay circuits for temperature sensor integrated circuit (IC). This sensor is utilized to gauge the circulatory strain and temperature of the patients. Figure 6.5 monitors blood crushing part and temperature sensor.

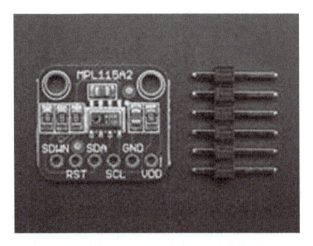

FIGURE 6.5   Blood pressure and temperature sensor.

FIGURE 6.6   Raspberrypi3.

d.   RaspberryPi3

The Raspberry Pi board is furnished with an SD card, and this space rewards us for introducing an SD card so we can utilize it as our device. The SD card is the focal stockpiling of the Raspberry Pi board, like the hard plate ring of a PC. The Linux bootable working framework is reasonable for this card, and should be utilized. Raspberry Pi upholds a Linux, Qtonpi, ARM, and Mac framework. You can pick the working framework; you need to utilize the Disk Chief application to play out this procedure on the SD card. You can likewise utilize another edge part, for example, an outer USB hard drive or USB streak drive. Raspberry Pi 3 is associated with WLAN (Figure 6.6, Raspberry Pi). We utilize this Raspberry Pi regulator to send patient information values to the cloud.

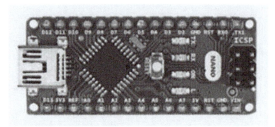

FIGURE 6.7   Arduino nano.

e) Arduino Nano

Arduino is a miniature regulator-based programming bundle. Because of its underlying open source equipment, it may very well be utilized straightforwardly when bought from a seller or made with parts at home. Various gadgets work (see Figure 6.7: Arduino nano). We utilize this Arduino to effortlessly change the information.

6.4   DATA COLLECTION

In this part, we attempt to depict the informational collection employed as the contribution of the classifier carried out utilizing different calculations. Information arrangement is a significant advance in grouping information as typical or diabetic. Counting the records of 73 diabetic patients (50 men and 23 women) in a 70-day period, a normal of three estimations were required a day. In this examination, we utilized six order calculations (NB [13,14], RForest [15], OR [16] and SMO (Minimum Sequence Optimization)) [17] [18–36]. In this examination, different arrangement calculations were utilized to characterize glucose information in a similar information extraction program. The blood glucose record contains six ascribes and 12,342 blood glucose records. Figure 6.8 shows the blood glucose estimation of a diabetic patient three times each day.

This part discusses the critical and the fundamental development of AI computations to accumulate and deal with the data. Table 6.1 presents the data set used. The data set used a database containing data on a couple of diabetic patients. We used this data set to endeavor the inimitable AI computations to distinguish and make estimates of diabetes. The data set fused the going with credits: sexual orientation, day the activities were insulin used, interior warmth level, and genuine work.

In this examination, we utilized some customized learning procedures to choose the most agreeable score to set the assumptions for diabetic patients. The accompanying cluster procedures were utilized in this test: Bayes, J48, Sequential Minor Improvement (SMO), Zero R, OneR, straightforward estimation and irregular backwoods. These investigations were directed utilizing Weka programming The informational index utilized for testing incorporates 12,367 data assessments.

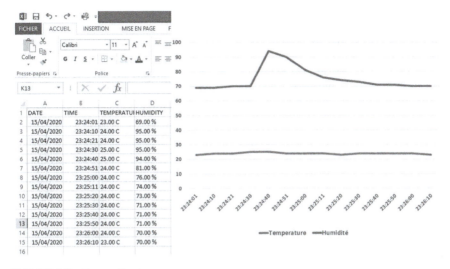

FIGURE 6.8 Data collection.

TABLE 6.1
Glucose, Temperature, Physical Activity

Day	Morning	Afternoon	Evening	Temp	No of ste
1	96	99	121	37	4324
2	154	68	78	38	6512
3	100	123	71	36	7852
4	123	87	111	37	5617
5	168	96	109	36	3587
6	145	121	86	38	4521
7	84	100	98	38	4968
8	92	108	123	37	5871
9	85	78	145	36	7689
10	62	68	167	37	6841

6.5 RESULTS

This section presents the results of research and discussion related to accuracy and receiver performance (ROC). Table 6.2 shows the accuracy and training time of various algorithms used, namely H regression, decision tree, K-means, classification and C4.5 (CART) algorithms (Figure 6.9).

Figure 6.10 shows the lead time for processing each order. The basic calculation is the longest calculation (1.56 seconds), while the shortest one is OneR, with a period of about 0.01 second.

Table 6.3 shows different parameters such as +ve rate and −ve rate, P rate, R rate and F-Rate calculated from our results.

TABLE 6.2
Accuracy Level of the Algorithms

Algorithms	Correctly Classified Instances	Incorrectly Classified Instances	Training Time (s)
NB	85.12%	18.54%	0.05
J Alg	74.23%	0.38%	0.12
0 R Alg	54.89%	16.56%	1.05
SMO	45.21%	25.35%	0.06
One R	89.14%	0.39%	0.02
Sampling	92.14%	17.03%	1.48
Regression (For)	96.18%	0.41%	1.02

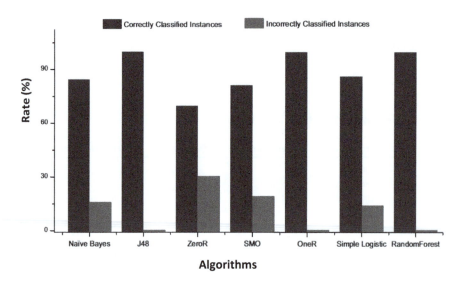

FIGURE 6.9 Correctly separated algorithms.

TABLE 6.3
Values of +Ve (TP), −Ve (FP) Algorithms

Algorithms	+Ve Rate	−Ve Rate	Pr Rate	R Rate	F Rate
NB	0.8692	0.3258	0.8217	0.8754	0.8745
J Alg	0.7456	0.008	0.6587	0.7412	0.7845
0 R Alg	0.8635	0.2547	0.7412	0.6878	0.2478
SMO	0.4532	0.3658	0.896	0.8635	0.6358
One R	0.6872	0.2147	0.5741	0.4756	0.9654
Sampling	0.5647	0.1117	0.5874	0.7412	0.8314
Regression (For)	0.3658	0.006	0.5859	0.5874	0.8741

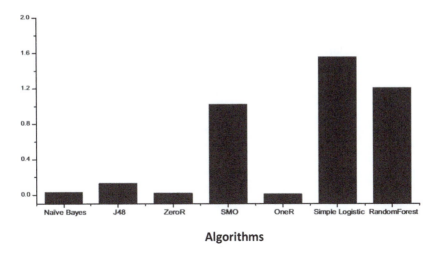

FIGURE 6.10   Training results for the different algorithms.

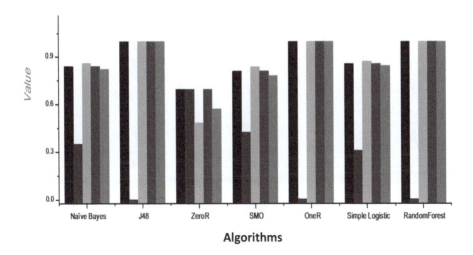

FIGURE 6.11   +Ve (TP), −Ve, PRate time results for the different algorithms.

Figure 6.11 shows different parameters such as +ve rate and −ve rate, P rate, R rate for different algorithms.

Contributions

Table 6.4 shows the upsides of particularity, affectability, exactness and accuracy for the calculations utilized in this examination.

Figure 6.12 shows the explicitness, affectability, exactness and accuracy of the various calculations. Concerning explicitness, affectability, exactness and accuracy, OneR, Random Forest and SMO are the calculations that arrive at the best outcomes.

TABLE 6.4
Values of Particularity, Affectability, Exactness and Accuracy FOR THE Algorithms

Algorithms	Particularity	Affectability	Exactness	P Rate
NB	48.5%	99.1%	85.1%	82.1%
J Alg	36.7%	100%	89.2%	89.3%
0 R Alg	78.8%	99.8%	78.3%	98.3%
SMO	58.5%	100%	65.4%	86%
One R	75.1%	99.2%	98.3%	78.2%
Sampling	68.2%	99.5%	85.9%	83.4%
Regreesion (For)	78.1%	99.0%	96.2%	86.2%

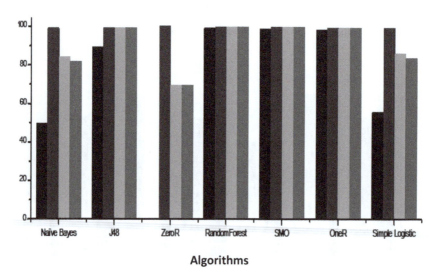

Algorithms

FIGURE 6.12　Specificity, sensitivity, accuracy, and precision of the different algorithms.

6.6　CONCLUSION

In this investigation, some AI computations are utilized to bunch data in the record. Subsequently, we utilized four principle estimations in this examination: OneR, Random Forest, SMO and naive Bayes of the diabetes dataset. It is utilized in tries different things with WEKA hardware to predict data about diabetic patients (Figure 6.13). We endeavor to keep up the capacity and feasibility of the referenced computations as far as exactness, accuracy and adequacy. The fundamental objective is to choose the most exact component. The irregular backwoods score exhibition for diabetes expectation is superior to SMO, OneR and naive Bayes scores. Future work will zero in on joining various techniques in the model, which are utilized to change the limits of the model to get higher precision.

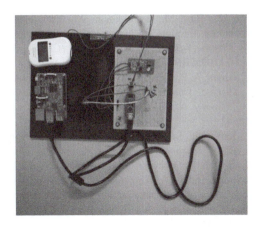

FIGURE 6.13   Overall kit.

REFERENCES

[1] Rghioui, A.; Lloret, J.; Parra, L.; Sendra, S.; Oumnad, A. Glucose Data Classification for Diabetic Patient Monitoring. *Applied Sciences* 2019, 9, 4459.

[2] Ruffini, M. Multidimensional Convergence in Future 5G Networks. *Journal of Lightwave Technology* 2017, 35, 535–549.

[3] Bernard, S.; Nuiro, S.P.; Pietrus, A. Diabetes, Complications and Limit Cycles. *Applied Mathematics E-Notes* 2015, 15, 197–206.

[4] Zhang, Z.; Zhan, Q.; Xie, X. Numerical Study on Stochastic Diabetes Mellitus Model with Additive Noise. *Computational and Mathematical Methods in Medicine* 2019, 2019, 5409180.

[5] Ahad, A.; Tahir, M.; Yau, K.A. 5G-Based Smart Healthcare Network: Architecture, Taxonomy, Challenges and Future Research Directions. *IEEE Access* 2019, 7, 100747–100762.

[6] Lloret, J.; Parra, L.; Taha, M.; Tomás, J. An Architecture and Protocol for Smart Continuous eHealth Monitoring Using 5G. *Computer Networks* 2017, 129, 340–351.

[7] Chen, M.; Yang, J.; Zhou, J.; Hao, Y.; Zhang, J.; Youn, C.-H. 5G-Smart Diabetes: Toward Personalized Diabetes Diagnosis with Healthcare Big Data Clouds. *IEEE Communications Magazine* 2018, 56, 16–23.

[8] Xiao, F.; Miao, Q.; Xie, X.; Sun, L.; Wang, R. Indoor Anti-Collision Alarm System Based on Wearable Internet of Things for Smart Healthcare. *IEEE Communications Magazine* 2018, 56, 53–59.

[9] Goyal, A.; Hossain, G.; Chatrati, S.P.; Bhattacharya, S.; Bhan, A.; Gaurav, D.; Tiwari, S.M. Smart Home Health Monitoring System for Predicting Type 2 Diabetes and Hypertension. *Journal of King Saud University—Computer and Information Sciences* 2020. www.sciencedirect.com/science/article/pii/S1319157819316076

[10] Najm, I.A.; Hamoud, A.K.; Lloret, J.; Bosch, I. Machine Learning Prediction Approach to Enhance Congestion Control in 5G IoT Environment. *Electronics* 2019, 8(6), 607.

[11] Ahmed, H.B.; Serener, A. Effects of External Factors in CGM Sensor Glucose Concentration Prediction. *Procedia Computer Science* 2016, 102, 623–629.

[12] Kannadasan, K.; Edla, D.R.; Kuppili, V. Type 2 Diabetes Data Classification Using Stacked Autoencoders. *Clinical Epidemiology and Global Health* 2019, 7(4), 530–535.

[13] Abbas, H.; Alic, L.; Rios, M.; Abdul-Ghani, M.; Qaraqe, K. Predicting Diabetes in Healthy Population through Machine Learning. *2019 IEEE 32nd International Symposium on Computer-Based Medical Systems (CBMS)*, 2019 (June), 567–570. https://doi.org/10.1109/CBMS.2019.00117

[14] Al-Zebari, A.; Sengur, A. Performance Comparison of Machine Learning Techniques on Diabetes Disease Detection. *1st International Informatics and Software Engineering Conference (UBMYK)*, 2019, 1–4. https://doi.org/10.1109/UBMYK48 245.2019.8965542

[15] Bandaru, S.R.; Kamepalli, S. (2019). Artificial Intelligence: Applications, Framework and Concerns-BFSI. *Journal of Advanced Research in Dynamical and Control Systems* 2019, 11(9). https://doi.org/10.5373/JARDCS/V11I9/20192766

[16] Driss, K.; Boulila, W.; Batool, A.; Ahmad, J. (2020). A Novel Approach for Classifying Diabetes' Patients Based on Imputation and Machine Learning. *2020 International Conference on UK-China Emerging Technologies, UCET*, 2020, 14–17. https://doi.org/10.1109/UCET51115.2020.9205378

[17] Hasan, M.K.; Alam, M.A.; Das, D.; Hossain, E.; Hasan, M. Diabetes Prediction Using Ensembling of Different Machine Learning Classifiers. *IEEE Access* 2020, 8, 76516–76531. https://doi.org/10.1109/ACCESS.2020.2989857

[18] Jacob, S.M.; Raimond, K.; Kanmani, D. Associated Machine Learning Techniques Based on Diabetes Based Predictions. *2019 International Conference on Intelligent Computing and Control Systems (ICCS)*, 2019, 1445–1450. https://doi.org/10.1109/ICCS45141.2019.9065411

[19] Thillaiarasu, N.; Gowthaman, N.; Chenthur Pandian, S. Design of a Confidentiality Model Using Semantic-Based Information Segmentation (SBIS) and Scattered Storage in Cloud Computing. In: Nath Sur, S.; Balas, V.E.; Bhoi, A.K., Nayyar, A. (eds.) *IoT and IoE Driven Smart Cities*. EAI/Springer Innovations in Communication and Computing, 183–213, 2022, Springer, Cham. https://doi.org/10.1007/978-3-030-82715-1_9

[20] Malini P.; Gowthaman N.; Gautami A.; Thillaiarasu N. Internet of Everything (IoE) in Smart City Paradigm Using Advanced Sensors for Handheld Devices and Equipment. In: Nath Sur, S.; Balas, V.E.; Bhoi, A.K.; Nayyar, A. (eds.) *IoT and IoE Driven Smart Cities*. EAI/Springer Innovations in Communication and Computing, 121–141, 2022, Springer, Cham. https://doi.org/10.1007/978-3-030-82715-1_6

[21] Thillaiarasu N.; Pandian S.C.; Gowthaman N. Novel Heuristic Scheme to Enforce Safety and Confidentiality Using Feature-Based Encryption in Multi-cloud Environment (MCE). In: Guarda, T.; Anwar, S.; Leon, M.; Mota Pinto, F.J. (eds.) *Information and Knowledge in Internet of Things*. EAI/Springer Innovations in Communication and Computing, 441–456, 2022, Springer, Cham. https://doi.org/10.1007/978-3-030-75123-4_20

[22] Preethi, P. et al. An Effective Digit Recognition Model Using Enhanced Convolutional Neural Network Based Chaotic Grey Wolf Optimization. *Journal of Intelligent & Fuzzy Systems* 2021, 41(2), 3727–3737.

[23] Thillaiarasu, N.; Pandian, S.C.; Vijayakumar, V. et al. Designing a Trivial Information Relaying Scheme for Assuring Safety in Mobile Cloud Computing Environment. *Wireless Networks* 2021, 27, 5477–5490. https://doi.org/10.1007/s11276-019-02113-4

[24] Thillaiarasu, N.; Chenthur Pandian, S. A Novel Scheme for Safeguarding Confidentiality in Public Clouds for Service Users of Cloud Computing. *Cluster Computing* 2019, 22, 1179–1188. https://doi.org/10.1007/s10586-017-1178-8

[25] Shyamambika, N.; Thillaiarasu, N. A Survey on Acquiring Integrity of Shared Data with Effective User Termination in the Cloud. *2016 10th International Conference*

on *Intelligent Systems and Control (ISCO)*, 2016, 1–5, https://doi.org/ 10.1109/ ISCO.2016.7726893.

[26] Thillaiarasu, N.; Chenthur Pandian, S. Enforcing Security and Privacy over Multi-Cloud Framework Using Assessment Techniques. *2016 10th International Conference on Intelligent Systems and Control (ISCO)*, 2016, 1–5, https://doi.org/10.1109/ ISCO.2016.7727001.

[27] Shyamambika, N.; Thillaiarasu, N. Attaining Integrity, Secured Data Sharing and Removal of Misbehaving Client in the Public Cloud Using an External Agent and Secure Encryption Technique. *Advances in Natural and Applied Sciences* 2016, 10(9 SE), 421–432.

[28] Kohli, P.S.; Arora, S. (2018). Application of Machine Learning in Disease Prediction. *2018 4th International Conference on Computing Communication and Automation, ICCCA*, 2018, 2018–2021. https://doi.org/10.1109/CCAA.2018.8777449

[29] Mir, A.; Dhage, S.N. (2018). Diabetes Disease Prediction Using Machine Learning on Big Data of Healthcare. *Proceedings—2018 4th International Conference on Computing, Communication Control and Automation, ICCUBEA*, 2018. https://doi. org/10.1109/ICCUBEA.2018.8697439

[30] Rout, M.; Kaur, A. Prediction of Diabetes Risk Based on Machine Learning Techniques. *Proceedings of International Conference on Intelligent Engineering and Management, ICIEM* 2020, 246–251. https://doi.org/10.1109/ICIEM48762.2020.9160276

[31] Saha, P.K.; Patwary, N.S.; Ahmed, I. A Widespread Study of Diabetes Prediction Using Several Machine Learning Techniques. *2019 22nd International Conference on Computer and Information Technology, ICCIT 2019*, (December), 18–20. https://doi. org/10.1109/ICCIT48885.2019.9038559

[32] Sarwar, M.A.; Kamal, N.; Hamid, W.; Shah, M.A. Prediction of Diabetes Using Machine Learning Algorithms in Healthcare. *2018 24th IEEE International Conference on Automation and Computing: Improving Productivity through Automation and Computing (ICAC)*, 2018 (September), 6–7. https://doi.org/10.23919/ IConAC.2018.8748992

[33] Sonar, P.; Jaya Malini, K. Diabetes Prediction Using Different Machine Learning Approaches. *Proceedings of the 3rd International Conference on Computing Methodologies and Communication*, ICCMC, 2019, 367–371. https://doi.org/ 10.1109/ICCMC.2019.8819841

[34] Sujatha, K.; Srinivasa Rao, B. Recent Applications of Machine Learning: A Survey. *International Journal of Innovative Technology and Exploring Engineering (IJITEE)* 2019, 8(6C2), 263–267. Retrieval Number: F10510486C219 & Sciences Publication /19©BEIESP.

[35] Tripathi, G.; Kumar, R. Early Prediction of Diabetes Mellitus Using Machine Learning. *ICRITO 2020—IEEE 8th International Conference on Reliability, Infocom Technologies and Optimization (Trends and Future Directions)*, 2020, 1009–1014. https://doi.org/10.1109/ICRITO48877.2020.9197832

[36] Vijiyakumar, K.; Lavanya, B.; Nirmala, I.; Sofia Caroline, S. Random Forest Algorithm for the Prediction of Diabetes. *2019 IEEE International Conference on System, Computation, Automation and Networking, ICSCAN*, 2019. https://doi.org/ 10.1109/ICSCAN.2019.8878802

7 Deep Learning Techniques Used for Detection of Disease in Tomato Plants

M. Rajesh Kumar[1] and K. Madhan[2]
[1]Department of MCA, Mailam Engineering College, Mailam, India
[2]Department of CSE, Mailam Engineering College, Mailam, India

CONTENTS

7.1 INTRODUCTION

The major factors that lessen food production include weeds, climatic changes, plant diseases, and so on. Extensive data shows that 80% of food production is carried out by small-scale farmers in developing countries like India [1] and, similarly [2], that 50% of yield reduction occurred due to the severity of pests and diseases. A plethora of methods have been developed to prevent yield loss caused by diseases. A preventive method at

DOI: 10.1201/9781003212201-9

the seedling stage is not sufficient to avoid epidemics; therefore, rigorous monitoring needs to be considered for early detection of disease in crops. In conventional farming, experts people are employed to visually inspect row by row to detect plant diseases, and it is time-consuming, labor-intensive work, and sometimes error prone as it is done by humans. Moreover, the availability of phytopathology experts is not constantly available, particularly in poor and segregation zones [3]. Regardless of the approach, the first crucial step is to identify the plant disease correctly for effective disease management. Precision farming is the new Agricultural Evolution, which can harness the power of science and technology to improve crop productivity. Precision farming aims at minimizing pesticides and fertilizers used to reduce overall farm expenses. It involves methods that can effectively detect and cure diseases or pests through precisely targeting the amount of fertilizer or pesticide respectively as required. As precision farming is shifting to new techniques from traditional methods, it has shown improvements in various sectors of agriculture. The sole purpose of precision farming is to get real-time data to increase crop productivity and maintain the quality of crops. The technologies that are used in precision agriculture are sensors and remote sensing, mapping and surveying, high precision positioning systems, variable rate, global navigation satellite systems, automated steering systems mapping, computer-based applications, and so on. The introduction of drones into precision farming practices has entirely changed the market. Drones can be used to achieve multiple objectives during farming including the sowing of seeds, the spraying of fertilizers and pesticides, and the monitoring of crop growth. To perform these activities, a drone must be equipped with a camera and sprayer with containers for pesticide/fertilizer. The drone can be employed to analyze crop health frequently and can detect abnormalities in the early stage. Drone-captured information (image/ video) can be analyzed in real time using a video/image analytics system based on machine learning or deep learning technologies to understand the crop growth pattern and predict the yield. Modern drones are equipped with a multispectral camera that is used in the estimation of vegetation indices.

Image processing has been adopted for more than two decades in the automation of certain agricultural practices. The images captured by remote sensing devices are used for the detection and classification of plant diseases. In recent years, deep learning techniques have been used in combination with plant disease detection in the leaves, fruits, and stems of plants. Deep learning uses several layers to extract high-level features from real-time input images without using hand-crafted features, and then extracted features are passed to different classifiers such as Knearest neighbors, support vector machines, and fully connected neural networks for disease classification. The present study aims at developing an automated mechanism for analyzing the images captured from simple camera devices in real-time using a combination of image processing and deep learning techniques and detect the four categories of tomato plant diseases, namely early blight, bacterial spot, septoria leafspot, and leaf curl.

7.1.1 TOMATO DISORDERS

According to the Food and Agriculture Organization of the United Nations census, nearly 170 kilotons of tomatoes were produced worldwide in 2014 [21].

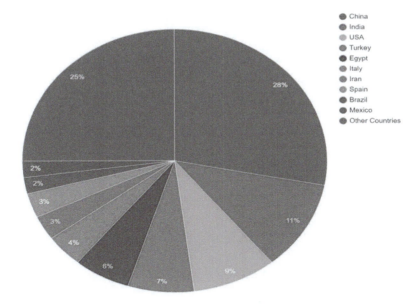

FIGURE 7.1   Worldwide production of tomato plant countries' tomato production in 2017.

Approximately 170.8 million tons of tomatoes were produced worldwide in 2017, whereas China alone produced 31% of the world's total tomato production. India accounted for 18.7% of the total production, as shown in Figure 7.1.

Diseases and pests that appear in fields can easily infect tomatoes. In addition to the fruit, pests and diseases affect other parts of the plant, which are the roots, stems, and the leaves. Generally, there are two plant substances that affect plant tomatoes, that is, living or biotic substances, including fungi, viruses, and insects causes bacterial spot, septoria leaf spot, leaf curl, early blight, fusarium wilt, leaf mold, mosaic virus, and powdery mildew diseases. Non-living or abiotic substances (Figure 7.2) encompass several environmental changes like high humidity, temperature change, poor soil pH, insufficient nutrients, and excess moisture. This work is carried out on Septoria leafspot, early blight, bacterial spot, and leaf curl.

7.1.2   PROBLEM STATEMENT

In this research, the problem addressed is to detect anomalies in the cultivated land, especially in disease detection in the tomato crop. Generally, plants are articulated bodies; however, a single model that detects and discriminates different diseases from plants can be very hard to define. The growth of a crop is not uniform and the variability in the intraclass between crops is increased because of their non-rigid structure. The research focuses on building an automated deep learning-based detection and classification of plant disease models that capture salient features of diseases and distinguish them from other objects of interest, that is, crops.

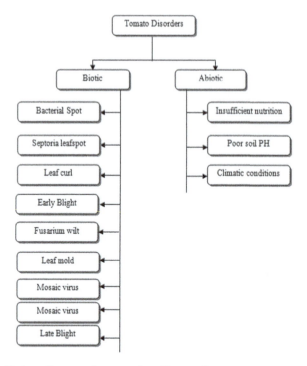

FIGURE 7.2   Various diseases of tomato plant: Tomato diseases.

7.1.3 OBJECTIVES

The objective is to propose a more suitable deep learning architecture to detect and classify tomato diseases, specifically early blight, Septoria leaf spot, bacterial spot, and leaf curl, by using a deep detector: faster R-CNN with "deep feature extractors" such as ResNet50. The objective is also to train and test the proposed system end-to-end on the tomato disease data set specified in this work, which contains comprehensive images of different tomato diseases, taken at early, medium, and final stages of infection status

7.2 LITERATURE SURVEY

This section analyzes numerous research studies carried out in pest and plant disease detection. Several studies have shown image-based evaluation methods are more reliable and replicable than visual human evaluation. In [3], the authors developed a method with image segmentation to measure disease severity on a black and white background, which reduces time for the measurement of disease severity and also eliminates human error. Many of these approaches to identify plant diseases based on images use the same basic technique. Firstly, pre-processing procedures used for background elimination and infected plant regions are segmented. This then extracts discriminative features for further study. Eventually features are classified for a particular task with supervised or unsupervised classification methods.

Assess [4] is an interative tool for estimating disease severity. The LeafDoctor app [5] is a smartphone app used to compute disease severity and also distinguish infected areas and healthy regions in color images. However, Assess and LeafDoctor applications are semi-automated since they rely heavily on hand-crafted feature extraction and threshold-based segmentation. It can therefore be hard to determine the correct threshold without human help to segment similar color lesions of different diseases. Automatic plant disease identification and disease severity are very promising in deep learning. Table 7.1 shows recent deep learning-based research work carried out on tomato pest and disease classification with positive results.

In [6], the authors extracted images of tomato leaves from the PlantVillage data set, which has 14,828 images distributed among nine classes of diseases (early blight, late blight, leaf mold, bacterial spot, leaf curl, Septoria leaf spot, spider mites, target spot, and mosaic virus). To eliminate hand-crafted features, the authors introduced a convolutional neural network (CNN) and trained classifier with raw input images. The authors analyzed the deep models (AlexaNet and GoogleNet) by visualization approaches, which recognize symptoms and classify disease lesions on leaves. Images

TABLE 7.1
Sample Images for Early Blight, Leaf Curl, Bacterial Spot

Disease	Symptoms	Begins	Sample
Early Blight	On leaves, Concentric diseased spots are formed with half-inch diameter.	In general, on older lower leaves, early blight starts and spreads to the plant. Gradually the infected leaves lose strength and die.	
Leaf Curl	No proper growth, upward curling of leaves, lesser leaf size, yellow tint on flowers and leaves.	Initial curling begins on lower leaves and rolls upward followed by an inward curl lengthwise	
Bacterial Spot	Appears on leaves as small (less than 1/8 inch)	First appears on middle of the leaf as yellow-green and darkens to brownish-red as they age.	
Septoria Leaf Spot	Several small diseased tan-edged spots in diameter 1/8 to 1/4 inches and filled with white center.	First appear on bottom of the plant on underside of older leaves.	

in the PlantVillage data set were taken under controlled conditions in a laboratory, which is a drawback of this model.

Authors [7] developed a CNN model with transfer learning and VGG16 for the identification of pest and disease in tomato plants. In original research, VGG16 was trained to identify 1,000 categories with 1.26 million images. The author collected 7,040 images from China that contain (leaf curl, leaf mold, late blight, bacterial spot, Septoria leaf spot, target spot, spider mites, gray spot, and mosaic virus, and healthy) categories with 640 images each. In order to identify different tomato diseases and pests, VGG16 extracts features from raw images and combines with SVM for the classification of diseases. The overall system performance relies, however, on fairly high-quality images but not low-quality images.

In [8], the authors collected 5,000 images from different farms in the Korean Peninsula. The author aimed to detect and identify tomato diseases and pest classes with locations in the images by seeking a better deep learning architecture. The authors considered faster R-CNN [9–13], SSD [14], and R-FCN [15–30] with various feature extractors (VGGnet, ResNet). Moreover, the authors suggested data augmentation to decrease false positives in training and to improve accuracy. The system was able to identify gray mold, pest, leaf mold, leaf miner, canker, powdery mildew, low temperature, nutritional deficiency, and whitefly. However, because of a smaller number of annotated samples, certain classes with large differences in patterns appeared to be confused with similar diseases and cause false positives.

The authors in [9] used 9,000 images of infected and healthy tomato leaves that had been taken in a laboratory to classify five diseases from a PlantVillage data set (leaf curl, bacterial spot, Septoria leaf spot, early blight and leaf mold). For data visualization, a full-color model was able to classify disease spots, while a gray-scale model learned leaf shapes and visual patterns of diseases. However, the full-color model achieved more accuracy compared to the gray-scale model. Images were taken under controlled conditions for the PlantVillage data set, which is a drawback of the model.

A diverse data set was used by the authors in [10] that includes images from a nursery, a farm, and the PlantVillage data set. In order to identify early blight, powdery mildew, and downy mildew, the author trained CNN. Using the Softmax activation function, a classification model is used to calculate disease classes' confidence score. All feature maps in previous layers are completely connected to the fully connected layer. The learned high-level features of a fully connected layer with Softmax function classify input images into powdery mildew, early blight, and downy mildew. Images were taken under controlled conditions for the PlantVillage data set, which holds a drawback of the model. A selection of 500 images from local fields and 2,100 images of tomato leaves on the internet were taken into consideration in [11].

The present authors used transfer learning in order to train CNN, in which leaves were graded as good, bad, and average in three categories for pest intensity in the Google inception model. By using transfer learning, the system execution speed is fast.

The authors in [17–20] collected 2,779 images from Google Images of hornworms, powdery mildew, cutworms, early blight, and whiteflies. Each disease category has

550 images, which is not substantial for training, and that also has an overfitting problem. Data augmentation techniques like vertical flips and random scale are used to overcome the overfitting problem. A CNN is effective for understanding image content, whereas training CNN from scratch requires extensive computing power and large amounts of data. To overcome these issues, the author did transfer learning on Google's inception model.

7.3   METHODOLOGY

The following section presents a more suitable deep learning architecture to detect diseases, specifically early blight, Septoria leaf spot, bacterial spot, and leaf curl in tomato plants. The aim of this research is to automate a deep learning-based tomato disease detection system to identify four different disease categories that affect tomato crops. Figure 7.3 specifies a brief summary of our proposed system. Moreover, a detailed description of individual parts in a tomato disease detection system is presented below.

7.3.1   DATA COLLECTION

The present authors collected a comprehensive data set of 1,090 real-time tomato leaf images infected by early blight, leaf curl, Septoria leaf spot, and bacterial spot. The images were taken by camera devices at different illuminations (lighting), times, different temperatures, and humidity levels and locations. Both authors visited

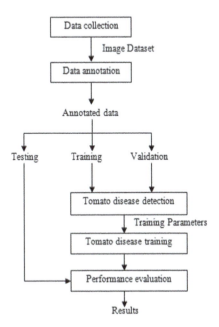

FIGURE 7.3   Brief summary of automated deep learning-based disease.

different tomato farms in Kallur, Mangapuram, and Piller in Andhra Pradesh, and added various types of data to our data set. We gathered the following data:

- 12MP, 48MP resolution images.
- Tomato disease images with different infection statuses (early, medium and final).
- Complex background (e.g., soil, stems).
- Images showing tomato plants infected with multiple diseases on a single leaf.
- Various sizes of tomato plants (initial, medium, and final growth sizes).
- Images containing partially blurred visual features of disease, or halfway or occlusion (disease is blocked or overlapped with leaves and stems of tomato plant).

The above factors help the proposed system detect and identify diseases at early, medium, and final infection stages and provide a confidence score for the disease along with the location on the tomato plant. Table 7.2 shows the symptoms and where disease begins in a plant and collected samples for early blight, leaf curl, Septoria leaf spot, and bacterial spot. The collected 1,090 images are resized into a uniform size of 800 X 600 pixels, 80% of the images were used for a training and validation set, and 20% were used for a test set, which contains a variety of images (early blight, leaf curl, Septoria leaf spot, healthy and bacterial spot at early, medium, and final leaf growth and also infection stages) in both the test and the test set, which makes our data set robust.

7.3.2 DATA ANNOTATION

Every image in our data set is manually labeled for the region, and contains a disease in a bounding box and the category to which the disease belongs, by using the labeling tool, which is a great tool for labeling images. Diseases such as early blight, Septoria leaf spot, and bacterial spot appear similar at an early stage; therefore, with the help of experts in the field, we obtained the required information needed to identify the disease category and infected regions visually in the images. The data annotation phase outputs different sized bounding box coordinates along with their respective disease category (ground truth boxes), which are then evaluated as Intersection over Union (IoU) with the system predicted bounding box (Table 7.1) coordinates from the testing phase. As the images were taken from the farm, they contain a complex background like soil, stem, and so on. Therefore, while securing the images, we need to collect them.

7.3.3 FASTER R-CNN TOMATO DISEASE DETECTION

The aim is to detect and identify four disease categories and locations in the tomato plant images. The bounding boxes that contain the disease should accurately define to which the disease belongs, to get precise results by the system. Faster R-CNN uses a region proposal network (RPN) to generate the required RoI's for tomato disease

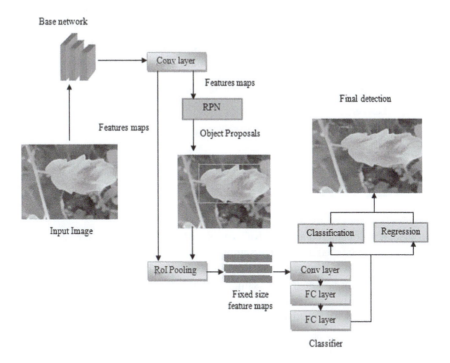

FIGURE 7.4   Faster R-CNN with ResNet50 tomato disease detection.

detection. The steps shown in Figure 7.4 steps were followed by Faster R-CNN tomato disease detection in an image:

- Pass input image to ConvNet and feature maps are returned to RPN.
- The RPN uses a sliding window on the obtained feature maps at each window and produces k fixed-size anchor boxes of different sizes and shapes in the tomato disease images. For each anchor, the RPN predicts the probability that an anchor is a disease and the bounding box regressor to better fit the anchor for disease.
- The ROI takes various types that have been obtained, the sizes of the bounding boxes (object proposals), and the crop in each proposal in such a way that each proposal contains tomato diseases and collects fixed-size feature maps to all the anchors.
- Eventually, feature maps are moved to fully connected a layer with a softmax and linear regression layer (Figure 7.4) and classify a disease category with the bounding boxes in a tomato image.

7.3.4 RPN Training and Loss Functions

The anchor box is marked "positive (disease)" sample only if the anchor box has an IoU greater than or equal to a threshold value of 0.5 with the ground truth box;

TABLE 7.2
Tomato Disease Categories with Total Number of Labeled Bounding Boxes that Tomato Disease Data Set Contains

Category	Total number of labeled Bounding Boxes
Leaf curl	1492
Septoria Leaf Spot	397
Bacterial Spot	1219
Early blight	630
Healthy	858
Total	**4596**

otherwise, it is considered a "negative" sample. Many anchors with the same growth truth box can be labeled as positive samples. For RPN training, neither positive nor negative anchors were ignored and this yields a mini-batch from a single image. When all anchors of an image were sampled, with a batch being made with 100 positive and 100 negative samples, if there were any insufficient positive samples, then they were padded with negative samples to form a batch data.

7.4   EXPERIMENTS AND RESULTS WITH DISCUSSIONS

The following section presents results achieved by the proposed system, which includes the tomato disease data set, experimental setup, quantitative results, qualitative results, failure analysis, and discussion.

7.4.1   TOMATO DISEASE DATA SET

The tomato disease data set consists of 1,090 real-time images from different farms located in Kallur, Mangapuram, and Piller in Andhra Pradesh, which were collected at different times, seasons, and various growing stages of disease (early, medium, and final). The Table 7.2 presents tomato disease categories and their total number of labeled bounding boxes, which are passed to train and test the proposed system. Each image includes one or more tomato disease labeled bounding boxes, which depends on the healthy category and the infected region in the tomato plant (Table 7.3).

7.4.2   EXPERIMENTAL SETUP

In order to perform the experiments, the tomato disease data set that includes four labeled tomato disease categories and a healthy class were divided into 60% for the training set containing 738 images, 20% for the validation set (176 images), and a 20% test set (176 images). To minimize an overfitting problem, the validation set is used, which is stated in the Pascal VOC challenge [16]. Training is performed first on

TABLE 7.3
Tomato Disease Detection Results
Achieved for the Proposed System Using
Faster R-CNN with ResNet50

Category	AP
Leaf curl	92.25
Healthy	88.57
Bacterial spot	81.41
Early blight	78.44
Septoria leaf spot	64.09
Total mean AP	**80.952**

the training set, and then on the validation set to evaluate the system. The expected results achieved with the unseen data (which is not seen by the system during training) from the test set are passed to our trained system for the final evaluation. The tomato disease data set was uploaded to Google Drive, and the training and testing process for the system was done in Google Collaboration, an online platform founded by Google that provides graphics processing unit (GPU) services for free of cost up to 12 hours in a single session.

7.4.3 QUANTITATIVE RESULTS

The automated proposed disease detection system identifies tomato diseases, specifically leaf curl, Septoria leaf spot, early blight, and bacterial spot in plants using a deep detector: Faster R-CNN with a "deep feature extractor" such as ResNet-50. In the first instance, performance is assessed with the IoU evaluation metric and average precision (AP) accuracy metric (Table 7.3) are used to evaluate the proposed disease detection system.

Tensorboard is an tensorflow [21] visualization toolkit provides value. Figure 7.5 shows a that precision x recall curve for (a) leaf curl, (b) healthy, (c) bacterial spot, (d) early blight visualization, and tracking of box classification loss, box localization loss, RPN objectness loss, RPN localization loss, and total loss. In Figure 7.6, the box classification loss is stable, starting high and going low and keeping around a value of 0.75 to 0.02. That the box localization loss, how actually the box should be closely located to the image where loss is maintained value between 0.05 and 0.01. Figure 7.7 shows RPN localization loss, suggestions for the boxes, and localization that it is related to. RPN localization loss is maintained at less than 0.01. RPN objectness loss is the actual kind of object (disease or not) that is found and how far from the result where RPN objectness loss is maintained at less than 0.01. Figure 7.6 shows the resultant loss curve for two-lakh epochs, indicating how well the disease detection system learned the tomato data and achieved less than a 0.1 error rate at 90,000 epochs.

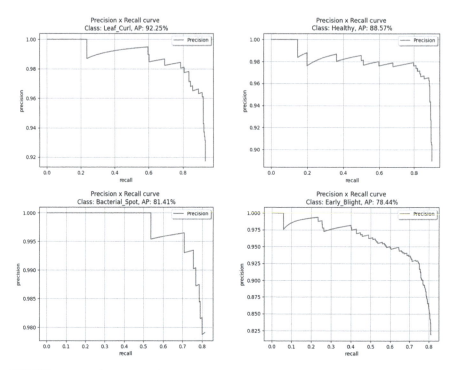

FIGURE 7.5 Precision x Recall curve for (a) leaf curl, (b) healthy, (c) bacterial spot, (d) early blight.

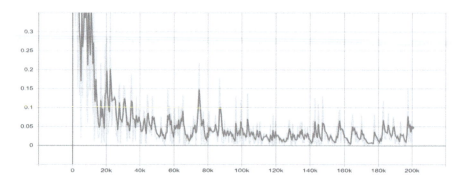

FIGURE 7.6 Box classification loss.

7.5 QUALITATIVE RESULTS

For every image in the tomato disease data set, the performance is evaluated for all the bounding boxes and the confidence score for leaf curl, bacterial spot, Septoria leaf spot, healthy, and early blight. The proposed system detects tomato disease categories with location in the plants at early, medium, and final disease stages. The system identifies diseases at the early stage in the plants shown (in Figures 7.8–7.11), so that farmers can

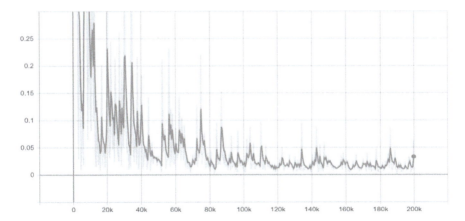

FIGURE 7.7   RPN localization loss.

FIGURE 7.8   Initial stage of leaf curl.

avoid severe crop loss in terms of quality and quantity. The proposed system trains with the front side of tomato leaf images; however, the system is able to detect diseases on the back side of tomato leaves, as shown in Figure 7.11, and also detects diseases that are in the out-of-focus distance (shown in Figures 7.12 and 7.13). The proposed system detects disease in a complex background (soil, stem, tomato), as shown in Figures 7.14 and 7.15 and also detects multiple diseases on a single leaf (see Figure 7.15).

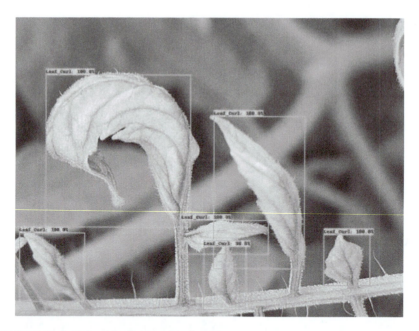

FIGURE 7.9   Initial and final stage of leaf curl.

FIGURE 7.10   Final stage of leaf curl.

FIGURE 7.11   Initial stage of bacterial spot.

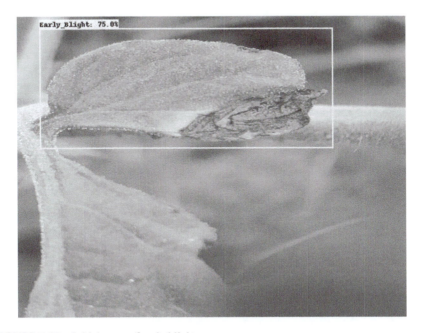

FIGURE 7.12   Initial stage of early blight.

FIGURE 7.13   Initial stage of Septoria leaf spot.

FIGURE 7.14   Complex background (stem & tomato).

FIGURE 7.15   Complex background.

7.6   CONCLUSION AND FUTURE RESEARCH

This research was focused on reviewing the efficiency of deep learning architectures for pest and disease detection in cultivated land. We collected a comprehensive data set of 1,090 real-time tomato leaf images infected by early blight, leaf curl, Septoria leaf spot, and bacterial spot, and the images were taken by camera devices with 12MP, 48MP resolution, under different illumination conditions (lighting), in all stages of tomato disease (early, medium, final), and given as an input to the proposed system. Different deep learning architectures were used to identify pests and diseases using deep detectors: Faster R-CNN, R-FCN, and SSD, combined with VGG Net and ResNet, AlexNet, and Squeeze Net. Based on a survey done on pest and disease detection, Faster R-CNN deep learning architecture combined with ResNet provided better performance compared to R-FCN and SSD. We propose an automated disease detection system using a deep detector: Faster R-CNN with ResNet is a feasible solution for farmers to detect early blight, leaf curl, Septoria leaf spot, and bacterial spot diseases located in tomato plants. We also trained and tested the proposed system end-to-end with our tomato disease data set specified in this work, which has 1,090 comprehensive images of early, medium, and final stages of tomato disease.

REFERENCES

[1] United Nations Environment Programme (UNEP) (2013). *Smallholders, Food Security, and the Environment*. Rome: International Fund for Agricultural Development (IFAD).

[2] Harvey, Celia A. et al. "Extreme vulnerability of smallholder farmers to agricultural risks and climate change in Madagascar." *Philosophical Transactions of the Royal Society B: Biological Sciences* 369.1639 (2014): 20130089.

[3] Barbedo, Jayme Garcia Arnal. "Digital image processing techniques for detecting, quantifying and classifying plant diseases." *SpringerPlus* 2.1 (2013): 660.

[4] Lamari, L. *Assess: Image Analysis software helpdesk, Version 2*, vol. 1. APS Press (2008).

[5] Pethybridge, Sarah J., and Scot C. Nelson. "Leaf Doctor: A new portable application for quantifying plant disease severity." *Plant Disease* 99.10 (2015): 1310–1316.

[6] Brahimi, Mohammed, Kamel Boukhalfa, and Abdelouahab Moussaoui. "Deep learning for tomato diseases: classification and symptoms visualization." *Applied Artificial Intelligence* 31.4 (2017): 299–315.

[7] Shijie, Jia, Jia Peiyi, and Hu Siping. "Automatic detection of tomato diseases and pests based on leaf images." *2017 Chinese Automation Congress (CAC)*. IEEE, 2017.

[8] Fuentes, Alvaro et al. "A robust deep-learning-based detector for real-time tomato plant diseases and pests recognition." *Sensors* 17.9 (2017): 2022.

[9] Ashqar, Belal A.M., and Samy S. Abu-Naser. "Image-based tomato leaves diseases detection using deep learning." *International Journal of Engineering Research* 2.12 (2018): 10–16.

[10] Khan, Saiqa, and Meera Narvekar. "Disorder detection in tomato plant using deep learning." *Advanced Computing Technologies and Applications*. Springer, Singapore, 2020. 187–197. https://link.springer.com/chapter/10.1007/978-981-15-3242-9_19

[11] Hasan, Mosin, Bhavesh Tanawala, and Krina J. Patel. "Deep learning precision farming: Tomato leaf disease detection by transfer learning." *Proceedings of 2nd International Conference on Advanced Computing and Software Engineering (ICACSE)*. 2019.

[12] Xie, Saining et al. "Hyper-class augmented and regularized deep learning for fine-grained image classification." *2015 IEEE Conference on Computer Vision and Pattern Recognition (CVPR)*. 2015, 2645–2654.

[13] Ren, Shaoqing et al. "Faster R-CNN: Towards real-time object detection with region proposal networks." *Advances in Neural Information Processing Systems*. 2015. https://proceedings.neurips.cc/paper/2015/hash/14bfa6bb14875e45bba028a21ed38046-Abstract.html

[14] Liu, Wei et al. "SSD: Single shot multibox detector." *European Conference on Computer Vision*. Springer, Cham, 2016.

[15] Dai, Jifeng et al. "R-FCN: Object detection via region-based fully convolutional networks." *Advances in Neural Information Processing Systems*. 2016.

[16] Everingham, Mark et al. "The PASCAL Visual Object Classes (VOC) challenge." *International Journal of Computer Vision* 88.2 (2010): 303–338.

[17] Llorca, Charmaine, May Elsbeth Yares, and Christian Maderazo. "Image-based pest and disease recognition of tomato plants using a convolutional neural network." *Proceedings of International Conference Technological Challenges for Better World*. 2018.

[18] Durmuş, Halil, Güneş Ece Olcay, and Mürvet Kırcı. "Disease detection on the leaves of the tomato plants by using deep learning." *2017 6th International Conference on Agro-Geoinformatics*. IEEE, 2017.

[19] Rangarajan, Aravind Krishnaswamy, Raja Purushothaman, and Aniirudh Ramesh. "Tomato crop disease classification using pre-trained deep learning algorithm." *Procedia Computer Science* 133 (2018): 1040–1047.

[20] Thillaiarasu N., N. Gowthaman, and S. Chenthur Pandian. "Design of a confidentiality model using semantic-based information segmentation (SBIS) and scattered storage in cloud computing." In: Nath Sur S., Balas V.E., Bhoi A.K., Nayyar A. (eds.) *IoT and IoE Driven Smart Cities*. EAI/Springer Innovations in Communication and Computing. Springer, Cham, 2022. https://doi.org/10.1007/978-3-030-82715-1_9

[21] Malini P., N. Gowthaman, A. Gautami, N. Thillaiarasu. "Internet of Everything (IoE) in smart city paradigm using advanced sensors for handheld devices and equipment." In: Nath Sur, S., Balas, V.E., Bhoi, A.K., Nayyar, A. (eds.) *IoT and IoE Driven Smart Cities*. EAI/Springer Innovations in Communication and Computing. Springer, Cham, 2022. https://doi.org/10.1007/978-3-030-82715-1_6

[22] Thillaiarasu N., S. C. Pandian, N. Gowthaman. Novel heuristic scheme to enforce safety and confidentiality using feature-based encryption in multi-cloud environment (MCE). In: Guarda, T., Anwar, S., Leon, M., Mota Pinto, F.J. (eds) *Information and Knowledge in Internet of Things*. EAI/Springer Innovations in Communication and Computing. Springer, Cham, 2022. https://doi.org/10.1007/978-3-030-75123-4_20

[23] Preethi, P. et al. "An effective digit recognition model using enhanced convolutional neural network based chaotic grey wolf optimization." 1 Jan. 2021: 3727–3737. IOS Press.

[24] Thillaiarasu, N., S.C. Pandian, V. Vijayakumar et al. "Designing a trivial information relaying scheme for assuring safety in mobile cloud computing environment." *Wireless Networks* 27, 5477–5490 (2021). https://doi.org/10.1007/s11276-019-02113-4

[25] Thillaiarasu, N., S. Chenthur Pandian. "A novel scheme for safeguarding confidentiality in public clouds for service users of cloud computing." *Cluster Computing* 22, 1179–1188 (2019). https://doi.org/10.1007/s10586-017-1178-8

[26] N. Shyamambika, N.Thillaiarasu, "A survey on acquiring integrity of shared data with effective user termination in the cloud," *2016 10th International Conference on Intelligent Systems and Control (ISCO)*, 2016, pp. 1–5, https://doi.org/10.1109/ISCO.2016.7726893.

[27] N.Thillaiarasu, S. Chenthur Pandian, "Enforcing security and privacy over multi-cloud framework using assessment techniques," *2016 10th International Conference on Intelligent Systems and Control (ISCO)*, 2016, pp. 1–5, https://doi.org/10.1109/ISCO.2016.7727001.

[28] Shyamambika, N., N. Thillaiarasu. "Attaining integrity, secured data sharing and removal of misbehaving client in the public cloud using an external agent and secure encryption technique." *Advances in Natural and Applied Sciences* 10.9 SE (2016): 421–432.

[29] Abadi, Martín et al. "Tensorflow: A system for large-scale machine learning." *12th (USENIX) Symposium on Operating Systems Design and Implementation (OSDI'16)*. 2016.

[30] Jacobs, I.S., and C.P. Bean. "Fine particles, thin films and exchange anisotropy." In: *Magnetism*, vol. 3, Rado, G.T. and Suhl, H. (eds.) (1963). Cinii.

Index